Environmental Science Experiments

EXPERIMENTS FOR FUTURE SCIENTISTS

Environmental Science Experiments

Edited by **Aviva Ebner, Ph.D.**

CHELSEA HOUSE
An Infobase Learning Company

ENVIRONMENTAL SCIENCE EXPERIMENTS

Text and artwork copyright © 2011 by Infobase Learning

Chelsea House
An imprint of Infobase Learning
132 West 31st Street
New York NY 10001

Library of Congress Cataloging-in-Publication Data
Environmental science experiments/edited by Aviva Ebner.
    p.cm.—(Experiments for future scientists)
Includes bibliographical references and index.
ISBN 978-1-60413-851-1
1. Environmental sciences—Juvenile literature. 2. Environmental sciences—Experiments—Juvenile literature. 3. Environmental Sciences—Studies and teaching (Elementary)—Activity programs. 4. Science projects—Juvenile literature. I. Ebner, Aviva. II. Title.
GE115.E595 2011
363.7—dc22
                                2010011204

Chelsea House books are available at special discounts when purchased in bulk quantities for businesses, associations, institutions, or sales promotions. Please call our Special Sales Department in New York at (212) 967-8800 or (800) 322-8755.

You can find Chelsea House on the World Wide Web at http://www.chelseahouse.com

All links and Web addresses were checked and verified to be correct at the time of publication. Because of the dynamic nature of the Web, some addresses and links may have changed since publication and may no longer be valid.

Editor: Frank K. Darmstadt
Copy Editor for A Good Thing, Inc.: Milton Horowitz
Project Coordination: Aaron Richman
Art Director: Howard Petlack
Production: Shoshana Feinstein
Illustrations: Hadel Studios
Cover printed by: Yurchak Printing, Landisville, Pa.
Book printed and bound by: Yurchak Printing, Landisville, Pa.
Date printed: May 2011

10 9 8 7 6 5 4 3 2 1

Contents

Preface

Educational representatives from several states have been meeting to come to an agreement about common content standards. Because of the No Child Left Behind Act, there has been a huge push in each individual state to teach to the standards. Teacher preparation programs have been focusing on lesson plans that are standards-based. Teacher evaluations hinge on evidence of such instruction, and various districts have been discussing merit pay for teachers linked to standardized test scores.

The focus in education has shifted to academic content rather than to the learner. In the race to raise test scores, some schools no longer address all areas of a well-rounded education and have cut elective programs completely. Also, with "high-stakes" standardized testing, schools must demonstrate a constant increase in student achievement to avoid the risk of being taken over by another agency or labeled by it as failing. The appreciation of different talents among students is dwindling; a one-size-fits-all mentality has taken its place. While innovative educators struggle to teach the whole child and recognize that each student has his or her own strengths, teachers are still forced to teach to the test. Perhaps increasing test scores helps close the gap between schools. However, are we creating a generation of students not prepared for the variety of careers available to them? Many students have not had a fine-arts class, let alone been exposed to different fields in science. We *must* start using appropriate strategies for helping all students learn to the best of their abilities. The first step in doing this is igniting a spark of interest in a child.

Experiments for Future Scientists is a six-volume series designed to expose students to various fields of study in grades five to eight, which are the formative middle-school years when students are eager to explore the world around them. Each volume focuses on a different scientific discipline and alludes to possible careers or fields of study related to those disciplines. Each volume contains 20 experiments with a detailed introduction, a step-by-step experiment that can be done in a classroom or at home, thought-provoking questions, and suggested "Further Reading" sources to stimulate the eager student. Of course, "Safety Guidelines" are provided, as well as "Tips for Teachers" who implement the lessons. A "Scope and Sequence Chart" and lists for "Grade Level" and "Setting" help the teacher with alignment to content standards, while the experiments themselves help students and adults think outside the paradigm of typical activities used in most science programs.

Science is best learned by "doing." Hands-on activities and experiments are essential, not only for grasping the concepts but also for generating excitement in today's youth. In a world of video games, benchmark tests, and fewer course choices, the experiments in these books will bring student interest back to learning. The goal is to open a child's eyes to the wonders of science and perhaps imbue some "fun" that will inspire him or her to pursue a future in a field of science. Perhaps this series will inspire some students to become future scientists.

—Aviva Ebner, Ph.D.
Faculty, University of Phoenix Online and
Educational Consultant/Administrator K-12
Granada Hills, California

Acknowledgments

I thank the following people for their assistance and contributions to this book: Mindy Perris, science education expert, New York City Board of Education District 24, for her suggestions and samples of experiments; Janet Balekian, administrator/science educator of SIAtech schools in Los Angeles, for experiment suggestions; Boris Sinofsky, retired Los Angeles Unified School District science teacher and mentor, for his evaluation of experiments; Dr. Esther Sinofsky, Director of Instructional Media Services for Los Angeles Unified School District, for assisting with research; Michael Miller, educator, and Cassandra Ebner, college student, for their help with the glossary and index; Aaron Richman of A Good Thing, Inc., for his publishing services, along with Milton Horowitz for always providing support and a personal touch to any project; and Frank K. Darmstadt, executive editor, Chelsea House, for his consistent hard work and his confidence in me.

This book is dedicated to Boris Sinofsky, science educatior and environmental science education pioneer, still teaching students in his "retirement." With over 40 years of service to education, he continues to captivate the imagination of children and serve as a mentor for all.

Introduction

The daily warnings in the media about pollution, climate change, and dwindling resources have opened the eyes of the general public to the importance of environmental science. Whereas in the past, such pursuits were in the realm of biologists, geologists, and meteorologists, more and more specialties have developed in environmental science over time. These include the study of specific species of plants or animals, changes in climate, historical science, paleontology, the study of changes in polar ice, and many others.

Our natural environment plays a crucial role in human social and economic life. We use the living world around us for food, energy, medicine, recreation, and industrial products. Nature offers both diversity and a choice. It is vital that humankind chooses to make better decisions in utilizing what the natural world has to offer. Progress has not come without a price. The pressure that humans currently place on the environment is greater than it has ever been in the past. Intensive agriculture has replaced more traditional forms of farming. Tourism has impacted mountain and coastal regions. Government policies related to industry have had a direct impact on rivers, coasts, and mountains. Dam construction, road networks, and other construction have played a role, too. Certain aspects of forestry management have resulted in a decline in biodiversity and soil erosion. Most notably, there has been an obvious reduction in the number of viable habitats for wildlife. With an increased exploitation of the natural world, there has been a clear reduction in wildlife habitat areas, species diversity, and animal population numbers. Over time, we will continue to see an increase in the loss of species of both flora and fauna. All of this is a result of humankind's destruction of land, air, and water quality.

However, even before reaching the stage in life when people determine their career path, we have the opportunity to be influenced and influence others in how we protect our environment. Children today are growing up with recycling bins, "green" products, hybrid cars, and other technology intended to protect the environment. Convenience has been replaced by conscience. The days of leaving the "problems" for future generations are long gone. The impact of years of tampering with and polluting the environment have taken their toll as habitats disappear and resources become scarce. From toxic wastes to oil spills, parts of the Earth have been contaminated or harmed to a large degree.

Fortunately, people today, especially children, seem more aware that we share this world with others. Native Americans have long held the belief that nature is to be respected. Their traditions retain close links with nature, acknowledged that all species play a role on the Earth, and assert that a natural balance must be maintained. They perceive the need for humans to live in harmony with the world around them.

The damage done to our environment due to lack of precautions is evident. The massive British Petroleum (BP) oil spill is perhaps the most notorious event of environmental damage in recent history. On April 20, 2010, the Deepwater Horizon oil rig exploded during drilling off the Gulf Coast, killing 11 workers and injuring 17 others. This extraordinary event occurred as a result of a methane gas buildup from the undersea oil well rising and igniting. As the well was blown open, a gaping hole left crude oil gushing into the ocean. Although the exact rate of the flow of oil resulting from the explosion is not known, estimates have been between 35,000 and 60,000 barrels of crude oil a day. As a result, an oil slick spread quickly over the surface of the water, eventually landing as tar balls on the sandy coasts of many Gulf Coast states. Oil plumes beneath the surface continued to spread. BP, which is in charge of this massive project, began efforts to slow or stop the leak. However, months later, though the flow was capped, oil continued to pour into the ocean, though at a much reduced rate. Months after the spill, the severe impact to the environment and wildlife was noted. There has been extensive damage to numerous marine habitats, despite crews working to prevent the spread of oil to local wetlands, beaches, and estuaries. Skimmer ships, containment booms, and barriers have been put into place but simply cannot capture all of the oil. Oil reached the shores of Texas, Florida, Mississippi, Louisiana, and Alabama. Though short-term efforts have been instituted to clean off tar-covered birds, sea mammals, and other marine animals, the long-term effects on ocean life are as yet unknown.

Environmental Science Experiments is a volume that will open students' eyes to the challenges we face today in balancing our use of resources with maintaining a healthy environment. As one volume in the multivolume Experiments for Future Scientists, *Environmental Science Experiments* will provide a glimpse into the study of environmental science and promote interest in children pursuing one or more areas as a career. Introductory paragraphs precede each experiment. Terms shown in italics in these paragraphs are listed in the glossary.

In "Oil Spills and the Environment," students will experience the challenges, on a small scale, of trying to clean up an oil spill and understanding its impact on wildlife, especially relevent because of the BP oil spill. Students further study the impact of people on the environment in "Acid Rain," "Slowing Down Erosion," and "Creating a Model Landfill."

On the other hand, students also have the opportunity to learn about positive ways they can affect the planet by finding out "What Nature Recycles," which entails discovering what does and does not degrade in a landfill; how to build a "Solar Still" for distilling water using only solar energy; "Filtering Water to Prevent Pollution," which discusses pollutants that may be contaminating your water; and "Investigating Alternative Fuels" as part of the search for replacing fossil fuels.

An appreciation for living organisms is also imbued through a "Biodiversity Activity" that demonstrates the diversity of organisms found in different parts of the world. Students learn about the role of rocks, soil, dirt, clay, sand, and water in "Soil Moisture and Permeability" and "Determining Soil Quality." "Desert Adaptations and Water" concerns how organisms survive in arid climates; "Succession: Forest in a Jar" allows students to observe how habitats can be created; "Dandelion's Habitat" demonstrates that organisms thrive in the right habitat; "Matching Animals to Their Biomes" tests the abilities of students to apply the knowledge they have learned about adaptations and environment; and "Studying a Freshwater Habitat" challenges students to take a first-hand look at a water environment and judge the impact pollution has made on it.

These and other experiments in this volume intend to increase awareness of the environment, the impact of environmental change on humans and other organisms, and how we can stop or slow the destruction of habitats. This book will serve as inspiration for students to pursue an education in a related field and one day contribute to saving our world. Today's students can be the saviors of our planet. As the Native-American proverb goes, "We do not inherit the Earth from our ancestors, we borrow it from our children."

Safety Guidelines

REVIEW BEFORE STARTING ANY EXPERIMENT

Each experiment includes special safety precautions that are relevant to that particular project. These do not include all the basic safety precautions that are necessary whenever you are working on a scientific experiment. For this reason, it is absolutely necessary that you read and remain mindful of the General Safety Precautions that follow. Experimental science can be dangerous, and good laboratory procedure always includes following basic safety rules. Things can happen quickly while you are performing an experiment—for example, materials can spill, break, or even catch on fire. There will not be time after the fact to protect yourself. Always prepare for unexpected dangers by following the basic safety guidelines during the entire experiment, whether or not something seems dangerous to you at a given moment.

We have been quite sparing in prescribing safety precautions for the individual experiments. For one reason, we want you to take very seriously the safety precautions that are printed in this book. If you see it written here, you can be sure that it is here because it is absolutely critical.

Read the safety precautions presented here and at the beginning of each experiment before performing each lab activity. It is difficult to remember a long set of general rules. By rereading these general precautions every time you set up an experiment, you will be reminding yourself that lab safety is critically important. In addition, use your good judgment and pay close attention when performing potentially dangerous procedures. Just because the book does not say "Be careful with hot liquids" or "Don't cut yourself with a knife" does not mean that you can be careless when boiling water or using a knife to punch holes in plastic bottles. Notes in the text are special precautions to which you must pay special attention.

GENERAL SAFETY PRECAUTIONS

Accidents can be caused by carelessness, haste, or insufficient knowledge. By practicing safety procedures and being alert while conducting experiments, you can avoid taking an unnecessary risk. Be sure to check the individual experiments in this book for additional safety regulations and adult supervision requirements. If you will be working in a laboratory, do not work alone. When you are working off site, keep in groups with a minimum of three students per group, and follow school rules and state legal requirements for the number of supervisors required. Ask an adult supervisor with basic training in first aid to carry a small first-aid kit. Make sure everyone knows where this person will be during the experiment.

PREPARING

- Clear all surfaces before beginning experiments.
- Read the entire experiment before you start.
- Know the hazards of the experiments and anticipate dangers.

PROTECTING YOURSELF

- Follow the directions step by step.
- Perform only one experiment at a time.
- Locate exits, fire blanket and extinguisher, master gas and electricity shut-offs, eyewash, and first-aid kit.
- Make sure there is adequate ventilation.
- Do not participate in horseplay.
- Do not wear open-toed shoes.
- Keep floor and workspace neat, clean, and dry.
- Clean up spills immediately.
- If glassware breaks, do not clean it up by yourself; ask for teacher assistance.
- Tie back long hair.
- Never eat, drink, or smoke in the laboratory or workspace.
- Do not eat or drink any substances tested unless expressly permitted to do so by a knowledgeable adult.

USING EQUIPMENT WITH CARE

- Set up apparatus far from the edge of the desk.
- Use knives or other sharp, pointed instruments with care.

- Pull plugs, not cords, when removing electrical plugs.
- Clean glassware before and after use.
- Check glassware for scratches, cracks, and sharp edges.
- Let your teacher know about broken glassware immediately.
- Do not use reflected sunlight to illuminate your microscope.
- Do not touch metal conductors.
- Take care when working with any form of electricity.
- Use alcohol-filled thermometers, not mercury-filled thermometers.

USING CHEMICALS

- Never taste or inhale chemicals.
- Label all bottles and apparatus containing chemicals.
- Read labels carefully.
- Avoid chemical contact with skin and eyes (wear safety glasses or goggles, lab apron, and gloves).
- Do not touch chemical solutions.
- Wash hands before and after using solutions.
- Wipe up spills thoroughly.

HEATING SUBSTANCES

- Wear safety glasses or goggles, apron, and gloves when heating materials.
- Keep your face away from test tubes and beakers.
- When heating substances in a test tube, avoid pointing the top of the test tube toward other people.
- Use test tubes, beakers, and other glassware made of Pyrex™ glass.
- Never leave apparatus unattended.
- Use safety tongs and heat-resistant gloves.
- If your laboratory does not have heatproof workbenches, put your Bunsen burner on a heatproof mat before lighting it.
- Take care when lighting your Bunsen burner; light it with the airhole closed and use a Bunsen burner lighter rather than wooden matches.

- Turn off hot plates, Bunsen burners, and gas when you are done.
- Keep flammable substances away from flames and other sources of heat.
- Have a fire extinguisher on hand.

FINISHING UP

- Thoroughly clean your work area and any glassware used.
- Wash your hands.
- Be careful not to return chemicals or contaminated reagents to the wrong containers.
- Do not dispose of materials in the sink unless instructed to do so.
- Clean up all residues and put them in proper containers for disposal.
- Dispose of all chemicals according to all local, state, and federal laws.

BE SAFETY CONSCIOUS AT ALL TIMES!

1. OIL SPILLS AND THE ENVIRONMENT

Introduction

On April 20, 2010, an explosion occurred on the deep-water oil rig known as "Deepwater Horizon," working for British Petroleum (BP). The consequences included 11 crewmen dead and the largest oil spill in history, causing the *Exxon Valdez* disaster of 1981 to pale in comparison.

Oil spills are a form of pollution that occurs when liquid *petroleum* products are released into the ocean. The oil might be *crude oil*, gasoline, *diesel*, or engine oil and is usually released from a *tanker* or ship, though oil can also leak from land sources. The impact on the environment and local *ecosystems* is often *devastating*. Birds may die from oil stuck to their feathers, impairing buoyancy, or from swallowing oil that they attempt to clean off their feathers. The fur of many marine mammals loses its ability to *insulate* when exposed to oil, causing those animals to die of *hypothermia*. Plant life in the ocean is affected when oil blocks sunlight from penetrating deep into the water, impairing the plants' ability to conduct *photosynthesis*. As plants die, the animals that eat them die, and fish that use them as shelter die. As the oil drifts over the water, more areas are affected. Therefore, one oil spill can *wreak havoc* on multiple ecosystems.

Oil spills cannot be reversed and are extremely difficult to clean up. In this experiment, you will create a model oil spill and determine the best method of cleaning it up.

 Time Needed

1 hour

What You Need

- ✎ aluminum cookie pan
- ✎ water, enough to fill the pan 2/3 full
- ✎ used auto oil, 1 cup (If not accessible, use a can of new auto oil)
- ✎ small rocks, about 15 to 20
- ✎ sand, about 2 cups (about 473 milliliters [ml])
- ✎ grass, a handful
- ✎ 4 feathers
- ✎ a few small pieces of wood or twigs
- ✎ dishwashing detergent, 1/4 cup (about 59 ml)
- ✎ rag
- ✎ laundry detergent, 1/2 cup (about 118 ml)
- ✎ fan
- ✎ paper, 1 sheet
- ✎ pen or pencil

Safety Precautions

Please review and follow the safety guidelines at the beginning of this volume.

What You Do

1. Place the rocks along one long edge of the cookie pan (Figure 1).

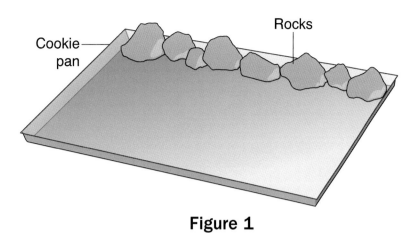

Figure 1

2. Add about 3/4 of the sand to the rocks to create a model of a shoreline (Figure 2).

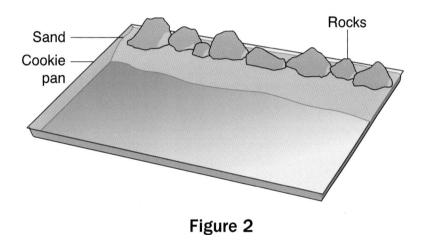

Figure 2

3. Add pieces of wood and grass to your shoreline to represent plant life, sticking them into the sand and between the rocks.

4. Add water by pouring it into the side of the tray opposite the shoreline. Fill the tray about 2/3 full with water.

5. Release the feathers into the water to represent the birds that live at the shoreline.

6. Pour the oil into the water to represent an oil spill.

7. Position the fan so that it will blow lightly across the water toward the shoreline (see Figure 3), and turn it on.

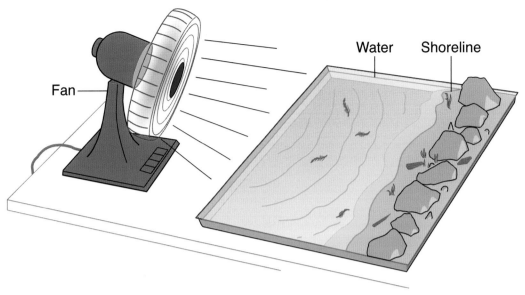

Figure 3

8. Observe what happens to the oily water, feathers, and shoreline.

9. Record your observations.

10. Try cleaning up the oil spill from the water and shoreline using each of the following items:

   a. rag

   b. dishwashing detergent

   c. laundry detergent

   d. remaining sand

   If necessary, add more water and/or oil as you test each cleaner shown on the data table.

11. Record your results on the data table. Record "yes" for effective, "no" for ineffective, and "partly" for partially effective for cleaning each of the areas listed on the chart.

Data Table				
Cleaner	**Shoreline**	**Water**	**Plants**	**Feathers**
Rag				
Dishwashing detergent				
Laundry detergent				
Sand				

 **Observations**

1. After observing the effects of the oil spill on the feathers and plants, how do you think an oil spill would affect real shoreline plants and birds?

2. Which method was least effective at cleaning each area?
   a. shoreline
   b. water
   c. plants
   d. feathers

3. Which method was most effective at cleaning each area?
   a. shoreline
   b. water
   c. plants
   d. feathers

4. What other methods do you think might work better?

Our Findings

Please refer to the Our Findings appendix at the back of this volume.

Further Reading

Fingas, M. *The Basics of Oil Spill Clean Up*. Boca Raton: CRC, 2000. A practical reference book on methods used to clean spills, impact of spills on wildlife, and a comprehensive glossary of terms.

"Gulf of Mexico Oil Spill Response," Deepwater Horizon Response. 2010. Available online. URL: http://www.deepwaterhorizonresponse.com. Accessed June 20, 2010. Up-to-date information about the BP oil spill.

Leacock, E. *The Exxon Valdez Oil Spill*. New York: Facts On File, 2005. A book for young adults explaining in detail about the spill, the clean-up efforts, and the impact on the environment.

"Oil Spills." Emergency Management. March 24, 2008. United States Environmental Protection Agency (USEPA). Available online. URL: http://www.epa.gov/oilspill/. Accessed September 23, 2009. From the USEPA, this article explains proper steps for oil spill clean-up.

Ott, R. *Sound Truth and Corporate Myth$: The Legacy of the Exxon Valdez Oil Spill*. Cordova, AK: Dragonfly Sisters Press, 2005. Overview of the Exxon Valdez disaster from a local resident's perspective and the legal battle fought by the victims.

————. *Not One Drop: Betrayal and Courage in the Wake of the Exxon Valdez Oil Spill*. White River Junction, VT: Chelsea Green Publishing, 2008. Told from the perspective of a Prince William Sound fisherman, the book discusses in detail the negative impact of the most famous oil spill in history as well as the legal roadblocks created by the oil company.

"Water pollution." *The Columbia Encyclopedia*, 6th ed. 2008. Available online. URL: http://www.encyclopedia.com/doc/1E1-watrpollu.html. Accessed September 23, 2010. Encyclopedia entry online for water pollution.

WAA. "Mapping the Response to BP Oil Spill in the Gulf of Mexico." 2010. Available online. URL: http://www.geoplatform.gov. Accessed June 20, 2010. Official government Web site tracking efforts to stop the BP oil spill.

2. ACID RAIN

Introduction

Acid rain is any *precipitation* that contains a high number of *hydrogen ions*, which lower the *pH* of the water to make it *acidic*. Acid rain is typically caused by *pollutants* that contain sulfur, nitrogen, and carbon. *Compounds* containing these *elements* react with *water vapor* in the air to produce acid rain. Acid rain, in turn, has a negative impact on plants, animals, and even structures. There have been many documented instances of buildings being worn away by acid rain. However, the greatest concern is the effect on living things. The United States Congress passed the Acid Deposition Act in 1980 to start assessing the situation. In 1990, the Clean Air Act was also passed. Since then, many studies have been conducted and more acts passed. The result has been a reduction in many dangerous pollutants. However, the problem has not been *eliminated*, just reduced. There are still lakes that cannot support certain types of fish because of the acidic nature of the water.

In this experiment, you will simulate acid rain and study its effects on plants.

Time Needed

20 minutes to prepare, 4 weeks to complete

What You Need

- 2 4-in. pots
- 2 rosemary plants

✎   potting soil, enough to fill the 2 pots

✎   vinegar, 1 bottle

✎   water, about the same amount as the vinegar

✎   pen or pencil

✎   paper, 1 sheet

✎   2 craft sticks

✎   black permanent marker

 Safety Precautions

Please review and follow the safety guidelines at the beginning of this volume.

What You Do

1. Add potting soil to both pots.
2. Plant a rosemary plant in each pot (Figure 1).

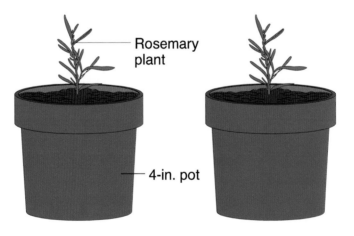

Rosemary plant

4-in. pot

Figure 1

3. With the black marker, write "Vinegar" on 1 craft stick and "Water" on the other stick.
4. Insert 1 stick into each pot (Figure 2).

Figure 2

5. Moisten the soil of the plant labeled "Vinegar" with the vinegar.

6. Add water to the soil of the plant labeled "Water."

7. Continue to moisten both plants daily with their respective liquids.

8. Record on the data table your observations about the plants over the next 4 weeks.

9. During the last week, remove the plants from their pots and observe their root systems.

Data Table				
Plant type	Observations, week 1	Observations, week 2	Observations, week 3	Observations, week 4
Vinegar plant				
Water plant				

 **Observations**

1. Vinegar is an acid. With that information, how did this experiment model the effects of acid rain?

2. What differences between the plants did you notice during the first 2 weeks?

3. What difference in root systems did you notice at the end of 4 weeks?

4. Since pollution contributes to acid rain, what did you learn from this activity about the effect of pollution and acid on plant growth?

Our Findings

Please refer to the Our Findings appendix at the back of this volume.

Further Reading

"Acid rain." *The Columbia Encyclopedia*, 6th ed. 2008. Available online. URL: http://www.encyclopedia.com/doc/1E1-acidrain.html. Accessed October 4, 2010. Encyclopedia entry regarding the effects of acid rain.

"Acid Rain." United States Environmental Protection Agency. 2008. Available online. URL: http://www.epa.gov/acidrain/. Accessed October 4, 2010. The official government site of the Environmental Protection Agency that explains the causes, effects, and measures being taken about acid rain.

Allaby, A., and M. Allaby. "Acid Rain." *A Dictionary of Earth Sciences*. 1910. Available online. URL: http://www.encyclopedia.com/doc/1O13-acidrain.html. Accessed October 4, 2010. A concise definition and description of acid rain.

Parks, P. *Our Environment—Acid Rain*. New York: Kidhaven Press, 2005. Children's book discussing what acid rain is, the effects on the environment, and what can be done about it.

Petheram, L. *Acid Rain: Our Planet in Peril*. London: Franklin Watts, 2002. Designed as an informational book for children, includes tips on how they can make a difference in reducing acid rain.

Wilkening, K. *Acid Rain Science and Politics in Japan*. Cambridge: MIT Press, 2004. A challenging book that attempts to explain developments in Japanese science regarding acid rain, as well as the politics involved.

3. SLOWING DOWN EROSION

Introduction

Erosion is the process by which soil, *sediments*, rocks, and other particles are removed from the *environment* and *transported* elsewhere. Erosion can be caused by water, wind, ice, or the slow downhill movement of soil. A related process is *weathering*, in which rocks are broken down (eroded) over time. People can speed up or slow down the process of erosion depending on how they use land. Planting trees and creating *terraces* in hillsides are two ways to reduce erosion. High rates of erosion can cause much sediment to build up in bodies of water and can negatively impact the *ecosystem*. In addition, large amounts of *runoff* can cause flooding and lead to deaths. Even animals can impair erosion (or have an impact on erosion). *Overgrazing* can reduce the number of plants that keep the soil from being carried away.

In this activity, you will simulate the reduction of erosion through the use of *vegetation*, then analyze your observations.

Time Needed

1 hour

What You Need

- empty plastic 2-liter soda bottle
- 2 square Pyrex® baking dishes
- watering can
- scissors
- soil from a yard or garden, about 2 liters

✎   4-by-4 post, 2 feet long (about 0.6 meters), found at a lumberyard

✎   sod, 4-in. x 10-in. section (about 10 centimeters [cm] by 24 cm), found at a nursery or landscaping department

✎   a bag of small plastic soldiers or cowboys, found at toy stores

✎   water, about 6 cups (about 1.5 liters)

✎   measuring cup

✎   paper, 1 sheet

✎   pen or pencil

Safety Precautions

Please review and follow the safety guidelines at the beginning of this volume. Be especially careful when using scissors.

What You Do

1. Using the scissors, cut off the neck of the plastic soda bottle (Figure 1).

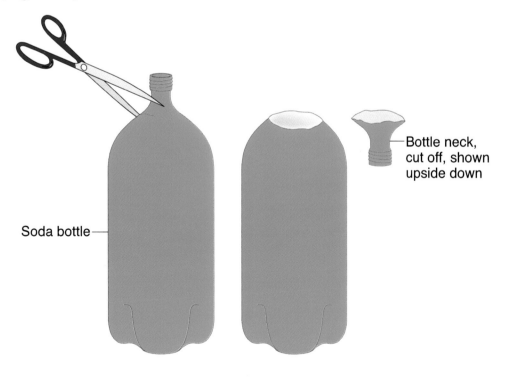

Soda bottle

Bottle neck, cut off, shown upside down

Figure 1

2. Then with the scissors, cut the plastic bottle in half lengthwise (Figure 2).

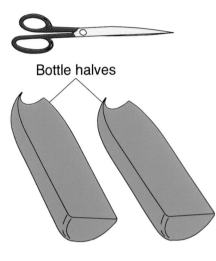

Bottle halves

Figure 2

3. Fill one-half of the bottle with soil.

4. Fill the other half halfway to the top with soil.

5. Cover the soil in the second half of the bottle with sod.

6. Place each of the 2 halves of the bottle into a baking dish.

7. With the wooden post, raise the bottom of each half by positioning the post just behind each baking dish so that the bottle halves are pointing down into the baking dishes (Figure 3).

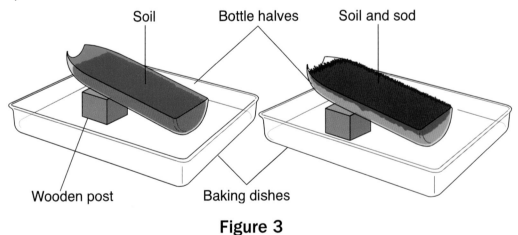

Soil   Bottle halves   Soil and sod

Wooden post   Baking dishes

Figure 3

8. Stand up some toy soldiers in each of the pans.

9. Add 3 cups of water to the watering can.

10. Water the bottle half that contains only soil.

11. Observe what happens to the soldiers in the collecting dish below.

12. Record your observations.

13. Pour the water from that dish into the measuring cup, and record how much water ran into the baking dish.

14. Record your observations about the amount of soil that ended up in the dish.

15. Repeat steps 10 to 14 with the bottle half containing soil and sod.

 **Observations**

1. Which dish ended up with more water runoff?

2. Which dish had more soil in it after the water was poured?

3. What happened to the soldiers in the dishes? What does this experiment simulate?

4. How do you think grass and other plants reduce erosion?

5. Evaluate the expected effects of adding rocks, sand, and small pieces of wood to this experiment.

Our Findings

Please refer to the Our Findings appendix at the back of this volume.

Further Reading

Bailey, Jacqui. *Cracking Up: A Story About Erosion*. Mankato, MN: Picture Window Books, 2006. Illustrated children's book explaining the process of erosion.

"Erosion." *The Columbia Encyclopedia*, 6th ed. 2008. Available online. URL: http://www.encyclopedia.com/doc/1E1-erosion.html. Accessed October 4, 2010. Article explaining how erosion and its causes occur.

"Erosion." *World Encyclopedia*. 2005. Available online. URL: http://www.encyclopedia.com/doc/1O142-erosion.html. Accessed October 4, 2010. Brief article regarding the definition and causes of erosion.

Olien, B. *Erosion (Exploring the Earth)*. Mankato, MN: Capstone Press, 2003. Children's book describing processes that occur on Earth, with a focus on erosion.

Palm, C., S. Vosti, and P. Sanchez. *Slash-and-Burn Agriculture: The Search for Alternatives*. New York: Columbia University Press, 2005. The author discusses the negative impact of slash and burn on the environment and other types of agricultural processes that can be used instead.

Ruf, F., and F. Lancon. *From Slash and Burn to Replanting*. Washington, D.C.: World Bank Publications, 2004. Based on field observations of how the farmers of Indonesia devised alternatives to slash-and-burn agriculture.

4. WHAT NATURE RECYCLES

Introduction

People across the country create tons of garbage. Actually, the United States Environmental Protection Agency (EPA) estimates that each person can produce more than 4 pounds of trash a day. Since hundreds of millions of people live in the United States, that is an enormous amount of garbage to be *disposed*. Some items break down naturally, while others may take hundreds of years. What to do with all of this trash is becoming an increasingly difficult problem to solve, as *landfills* become full and *contamination* from trash affects local *ecosystems*. The best solution is to reduce the amount of trash produced and use products that are *biodegradable*. However, even when we dispose of our trash, many of us put items that nature can *recycle* into the kind of bags that can take years to break down.

In this experiment, you will test various trash bags to determine if they are biodegradable, as well as examine the breakdown of the garbage inside them.

Time Needed

2 hours to prepare, 8 weeks to complete

What You Need

- ✎ brown paper grocery bag
- ✎ plastic grocery bag
- ✎ black or green plastic trash bag (e.g., Hefty®)
- ✎ biodegradable plastic trash bag

- 4 plastic bag ties
- scissors
- shovel
- several large pieces of wood
- 4 bricks
- 1 pair of latex gloves
- slice of bread
- peel from an apple
- coffee grounds, 4 tablespoons
- banana peel
- slice of cheese
- area of dirt in a yard or other outdoor area where you have permission to dig a large hole
- water, enough to wet the dirt
- pen or pencil
- lined paper, a few sheets

 ## Safety Precautions

Please review and follow the safety guidelines at the beginning of this volume.

What You Do

1. Identify the smallest of the four different types of bags—grocery and trash bags.

2. Cut the other three to the same length as the smallest one (Figure 1).

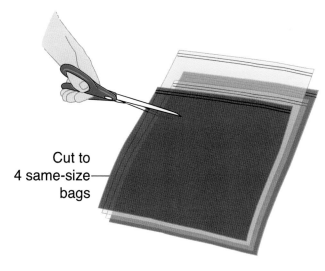

Figure 1

3. In each of the four bags, place the following:

    a. one-quarter of the slice of bread

    b. one-quarter of the apple peel

    c. 1 tablespoon of coffee grounds

    d. one-quarter of the banana peel

    e. one-quarter of the slice of cheese

4. Close each bag securely with a tie (Figure 2).

Figure 2

5. Dig a large hole in an area of dirt where you have permission
   to do so. It must be large enough to place all four bags inside,
   side by side.

6. Place the bags inside the large hole, laying them next to each other (Figure 3).

Bags with trash   Hole in the ground

Figure 3

7. Cover the bags with the dirt you dug out.
8. Water the soil so that it is wet over each bag.
9. Lay the pieces of wood over the wet dirt.
10. Place the 4 bricks over the pieces of wood to hold them down.
11. After 4 weeks, remove the bricks, the wood, and the dirt.
12. Wearing gloves, untie the trash bags.
13. Examine the contents of each bag.
14. Record your observations, including the state of decomposition of the bags, the contents of the bags, and any odors you smell.
15. Retie the bags.
16. Repeat steps 6 to 14.
17. Dispose of the trash and bags properly in a waste bin designated for the type of trash contained in the bags.
18. Refill the hole with dirt so that it is not a hazard to people walking there.

 **Observations**

1. Did any of the bags start to degrade?

2. What did you observe in each bag about the status of the contents? Were there any major differences in the contents of the different bags?

3. How do you think the choice of trash bags we use impacts the environment?

4. What suggestions do you have to speed up the breakdown of the plastic bags?

Our Findings

Please refer to the Our Findings appendix at the back of this volume.

Further Reading

Donald, R. *Recycling*. Danbury, CT: Children's Press, 2002. A book for children about the impact on the environment when recycling does not occur and how to recycle products and trash.

Lund, H. *McGraw-Hill Recycling Handbook*, 2nd ed. New York: McGraw-Hill, 2000. Provides comprehensive information on recyclable products.

"Municipal Solid Waste." United States Environmental Protection Agency. 2008. Available online. URL: http://www.epa.gov/epawaste/nonhaz/municipal/index.htm. Accessed October 18, 2010. The EPA's guidelines for non-hazardous waste removal and recycling.

"Recycling." *The Columbia Encyclopedia*, 6th ed. 2008. Available online. URL: http://www.encyclopedia.com/doc/1E1-recyclin.html. Accessed October 18, 2010. Entry about recycling and waste disposal.

Scott, N. *Reduce, Reuse, Recycle: An Easy Household Guide*. New York: Chelsea Green Publishing, 2007. Layman's handbook on what can be recycled, listed in alphabetical order.

Stevens, E. *Green Plastics: An Introduction to the New Science of Biodegradable Plastics*. Princeton: Princeton University Press, 2001. An overview of the chemistry of plastics and an introduction to the production and advantages of more environmentally friendly plastics.

5. SOLAR STILL

Introduction

People rely on water for survival, as do most *organisms* on Earth. About 71 percent of the Earth's surface is covered by water, most of it found in the world's oceans. Oceans are composed of salt water; humans need fresh water. In some parts of the world, fresh water is not easily *accessible*. However, salt water can be *distilled* to produce fresh water, and the easiest method of doing so is by using a *solar still*. A solar still uses the Sun's heat energy to *evaporate* water from a salt-water *solution*, then allows the water to *condense* for collection. This is also known as *desalination*. In *remote* communities or areas where a disaster has struck, this may be the most practical method for obtaining fresh water when *resources* are *scarce*. Some developing countries use this technique on a regular basis. However, quality of water collected depends on the water being distilled. If the water is *brackish*, the results tend to be poor.

Solar stills have a long history, with records going back as far as 2,000 years, though stills were once typically used to produce salt, not fresh water. The United States Navy used solar stills in life rafts during World War II.

In this experiment, you will build a solar still and a salt-water tester. You will use the solar still to collect fresh water and the salt-water tester to verify that the original source was salt water and that the water collected is fresh water.

 Time Needed

1 hour to prepare, 2 days to complete

What You Need

- ✎ large bowl
- ✎ small water glass
- ✎ plastic wrap, enough to cover bowl
- ✎ Scotch™ tape
- ✎ pitcher
- ✎ water, enough to fill the pitcher
- ✎ salt, 3 tablespoons (about 44 ml)
- ✎ small rock
- ✎ stirring spoon
- ✎ ruler
- ✎ 2 wooden craft sticks
- ✎ aluminum foil, enough to cover the craft sticks
- ✎ 9-volt battery
- ✎ electrical buzzer

Safety Precautions

Please review and follow the safety guidelines at the beginning of this volume.

What You Do

1. Fill a pitcher with water.
2. Add the salt to the water.
3. Stir the water until the salt dissolves.
4. Pour the salt water into the large bowl, enough to fill it with about 2 in. (5 cm) of water (Figure 1).

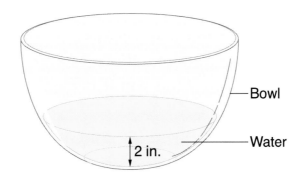

Figure 1

5. Place the empty glass into the bowl, making sure that the glass is taller than the level of salt water but shorter than the height of the bowl (Figure 2).

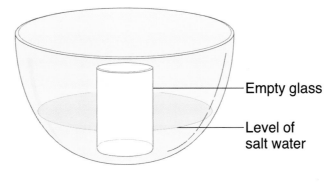

Figure 2

6. Cover the bowl with plastic wrap, and seal it tightly in place with Scotch™ tape.
7. Place a small rock on the center of the plastic wrap, directly over the glass, so that the plastic is weighed down in the middle.
8. Place the whole apparatus you have just made into sunlight outside.
9. Leave the apparatus outside for the entire day or for 2 days if you have enough time.

10. While your apparatus is left outside, build a salt-water tester, which will indicate if the water contains salt. Salt water contains ions that can conduct electricity and complete a circuit, so that the buzzer will sound. If the water is fresh water and not salt water, the buzzer will not sound.

11. Cover 2 wooden craft sticks with aluminum foil.

12. Tape the positive end of the battery to the red wire of the buzzer (Figure 3).

13. Tape the black wire of the buzzer to one of the aluminum foil–covered sticks (Figure 3).

14. Tape the negative end of the battery to the other aluminum foil–covered craft stick (Figure 3).

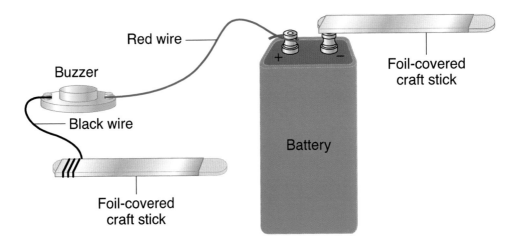

Figure 3. Salt-Water Tester.

15. Touch the 2 foil-covered craft sticks together to test your machine. If it buzzes, you connected everything correctly. If it does not, review the instructions and try again.

16. Once your salt-water tester is operating, remove the plastic wrap from your original apparatus and carefully remove the glass from the bowl. There should be fresh water inside the glass.

17. Stick the ends of both foil-covered craft sticks into the glass of water, holding the sticks so that the tips in the water are about 1 in. apart from each other.

18. Observe if the buzzer makes a sound.

19. Remove the sticks from the glass.

20. Repeat steps 17 and 18 with the salt water in the large bowl.

 **Observations**

1. Was the water in the glass fresh water or salt water?

2. How do you know your answer to item 1 is correct?

3. What else could you do to test the water in the glass to see if it is fresh water?

4. Why do people use solar stills with salt water?

Our Findings

Please refer to the Our Findings appendix at the back of this volume.

Further Reading

DeGunther, R. *Solar Power Your Home for Dummies*. Hoboken, NJ: For Dummies, 2007. Details the findings of Francis Galton, Darwin's half cousin, who is considered the father of biometry. Detailed how-to-book on selecting, building, and installing solar projects for the home.

"Desalination of Water." *The Columbia Encyclopedia*, 6th ed. 2008. Available online. URL: http://www.encyclopedia.com/doc/1E1-water-de.html. Accessed September 25, 2010. Article explaining the processes of desalination and distillation.

Gleick, P. *Water in Crisis: A Guide to the World's Fresh Water Resources*. Oxford: Oxford University Press, 1993. An environmental science reference book with a focus on water resources.

"Practical Answers: Water and Sanitation." *Practical Action.* http://practicalaction.org/practicalanswers/index.php?cPath=22. Accessed September 25, 2010. Gives information about the uses of solar stills, how they work, and background history.

Stikkerd, A. *Water: The Blood of the Earth—Exploring Sustainable Water Management for the New Millennium*. New York: Cosimo Books, 2007. Tackles the problem of finding or creating enough potable water for the world in the future.

United States Army. *Water Desalination*. Honolulu: University Press of the Pacific, 2005. A technical manual for processes that produce drinking water from sea water.

6. BIODIVERSITY ACTIVITY

Introduction

Biodiversity includes the variety of life-forms found in an *ecosystem* and is short for "biological diversity." Scientists often check on the biodiversity in an area to ensure that the *habitat* is not being affected *adversely* by any number of conditions. When biodiversity decreases, there is typically a negative factor that causes *species* to die off. When biodiversity is high, the area tends to be "healthy." Biodiversity can include *genetic* diversity, species diversity, and ecosystem diversity. Across the Earth, biodiversity is not equal in all areas. Some habitats support more biodiversity than others. Rain forests, for example, have a high rate of biodiversity. As rain forests are destroyed, the habitats that supported biodiversity disappear. As organisms lose their habitat, they often die, leading to a decrease in biodiversity in the area and increases to the list of species on the *endangered species* list.

In this experiment, you will model the biodiversity found in different *biome*s and compare their biodiversity to that of a typical lawn or wheat field.

Time Needed

45 minutes

What You Need

✎ 15 medium-sized glass jars

- large container of a big quantity (more than 100) of 15 different small, hard items (e.g., uncooked pinto beans, uncooked lima beans, sunflower seeds, dried peas, candy corn)
- 15 labels
- black marker
- pen or pencil
- paper, 1 sheet

Safety Precautions

Please review and follow the safety guidelines at the beginning of this volume.

What You Do

1. The 15 different items each represents a different species. Select 10 of the "species," and place 1 sample of each into a glass jar.

2. Select an additional 5 of the "species," and place 2 samples of each into that same glass jar (for a total of 20 "species").

3. Label the jar "Tropical rain forest" (Figure 1).

Figure 1

4. Repeat steps 1 to 3 three more times using the same items. These 4 jars will represent the vast tropical rain forests of the world.

5. Select 12 of the items, and place 2 samples of each into another jar.

6. Label this jar "Coniferous forest" (Figure 2).

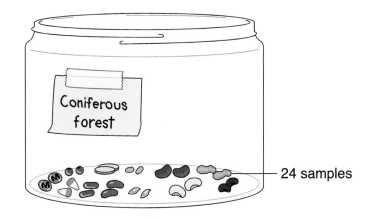

Figure 2

7. Repeat steps 5 and 6 using the same items. These 2 jars represent the coniferous forests of the world.

8. Select 12 "species," and place 2 samples of each into another jar.

9. Label this jar "Deciduous forest."

10. Repeat steps 8 and 9 using the same items. These 2 jars represent the deciduous forests of the world.

11. Select 7 items, and place 3 samples of each into another jar.

12. Label this jar "Desert."

13. Repeat steps 11 and 12 using the same items. These jars represent the deserts of the world.

14. Select 7 items, and place 3 samples of each into another jar.

15. Label this jar "Grassland."

16. Repeat steps 14 and 15 using the same items. These jars represent the grasslands of the world.

17. Select 1 item, and place 100 samples of it into another jar.

18. Select 1 item, and place 5 samples of it into the same jar.

19. Label this jar "Lawn or wheat field."

20. Repeat steps 17 to 19 using the same items. These jars represent a typical lawn or wheat field.

21. Complete the data table.

Data Table				
Biome or area	Number of species	Number of members of species	Total number of organisms	Biodiversity = number of species / total number or organisms

 Observations

1. Which biome had the greatest biodiversity (the largest number in the final column of the data table)?

2. Which had the least?

3. How is this activity a reflection of biodiversity in biomes?

4. The rain forests have been slowly disappearing due to deforestation. Based on this experiment, why do you think it is so important to save the rain forests?

5. When we destroy the natural habitat that exists in an area in order to plant fields, what impact does it have on biodiversity?

Our Findings

Please refer to the Our Findings appendix at the back of this volume.

Further Reading

Chivian, E., and A. Bernstein. *Sustaining Life: How Human Health Depends on Biodiversity*. Oxford: Oxford University Press, 2008. Provides information about the connectedness of species across the world.

Duffy, J. "Biodiversity." *The Encyclopedia of Earth*, 2007. Available online. URL: http://www.eoearth.org/article/biodiversity. Accessed October 18, 2010. Concise explanation of biodiversity, along with suggestions for additional reading.

Faith, D. "Biodiversity." *Stanford Encyclopedia of Philosophy*, 2003. Available online. URL: http://plato.stanford.edu/entries/biodiversity. Accessed October 18, 2010. Excellent Web site that provides a detailed background on the origins of the word *biodiversity*, as well as an overview of biodiversity around the world.

Lovejoy, T., and L. Hannah. *Climate Change and Biodiversity*. New Haven, CT: Yale University Press, 2006. Discusses global interactions and the impact of changes in climate on organisms around the world.

Maclaurin, J., and K. Sterelny. *What Is Biodiversity?* Chicago: University of Chicago Press, 2008. Discusses the definition of biodiversity, its importance, and how it is measured.

Patent, D. *Biodiversity*. Florida: Sandpiper, 2003. Children's book written from the author's personal experiences related to observing biodiversity around the world.

7. DESERT ADAPTATIONS AND WATER

Introduction

A *desert* may often seem like it should be *devoid* of life. This is because water is *vital* for life, and deserts receive very little or no *precipitation*. Deserts cover about 20 to 30 percent of the Earth's surface. *Mammals* rarely live in desert *environments* because desert climates do not produce the amount of water these mammals require for survival. Also, large animals find desert survival more challenging than smaller animals. Typically, *reptiles* are commonly found in deserts because of their ability to *conserve* moisture. However, despite its harsh conditions, a desert is full of life. There are numerous varieties of plants and animals that live in desert *biomes*. Their success is due to their *adaptations* to environmental conditions. Adaptations that help prevent water loss provide the best chances for survival.

In this experiment, you will model the effects of a desert *climate* on wet objects to observe the loss of water.

Time Needed

15 minutes to prepare, 24 hours to complete

What You Need

- 2 sponges, typical kitchen variety
- scale
- dish or pan
- label

✎   pen or pencil

✎   paper

✎   water, as needed from tap

✎   reference books or computer with Internet access

Safety Precautions

Please review and follow the safety guidelines at the beginning of this volume. Adult supervision is recommended when accessing the Internet. Follow all computer and Internet safety guidelines.

What You Do

1. Wet 1 sponge so that it is completely moistened but not dripping water.
2. Weigh that sponge (Figure 1).

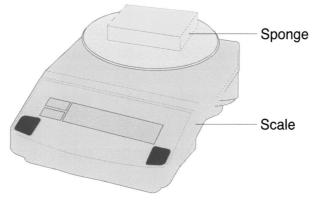

Figure 1

3. Record the results on the data table.
4. Set aside the wet sponge in the dish.
5. Label the dish "Control" (Figure 2).

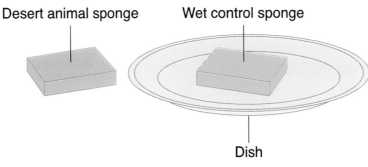

Desert animal sponge   Wet control sponge

Dish

Figure 2

6. Leave the control sponge out in the open, uncovered, for the duration of this experiment.

7. Wet the second sponge so that it is completely moistened but not dripping water.

8. Weigh the second sponge.

9. Record the results on the data table.

10. This sponge will be your "desert animal."

11. You must leave your desert animal out and exposed for at least 4 hours of the next 24 hours. Choose the time of day when you will leave out the sponge.

12. For the other 20 hours, keep the "desert animal" sponge protected from drying out. You may not put the sponge in a closed container, as a real animal would die from lack of oxygen. Be creative in your choices and try to model nature, i.e., by putting the "desert animal" in a hole in the ground.

13. After 24 hours, reweigh the control sponge.

14. Record the results on the data table.

15. Reweigh the other sponge.

16. Record the results on the data table.

Data Table		
Sponges	Weight at start of experiment	Weight after 24 hours
Control		
Desert animal		

 **Observations**

1. Which sponge lost the most weight in 24 hours?
2. Why do you think the sponges weighed less after 24 hours?
3. How did this simulate the challenges of organisms living in the desert?
4. Using reference books or the Internet, research the adaptations made by desert organisms that help them survive the lack of moisture.

Our Findings

Please refer to the Our Findings appendix at the back of this volume.

Further Reading

"Desert." *The Columbia Encyclopedia*, 6th ed. 2008. Available online. URL: http://www.encyclopedia.com/doc/1E1-desert.html. Accessed October 5, 2010. Encyclopedia entry that explains what constitutes a desert and what is found in a desert.

"The Desert Biome." University of California Museum of Paleontology. Available online. URL: http://www.ucmp.berkeley.edu/exhibits/biomes/deserts.php. Accessed October 5, 2010. Detailed information on the desert biome and the different types of deserts.

"Desert Plant Survival." Desert USA. 2009. Available online. URL: http://www.desertusa.com/du_plantsurv.html. Accessed October 5, 2009. Web site for traveling around the southwestern portion of the United States. Includes information on plant and animal survival in the desert.

Taylor, J., and D. Taylor. *Endangered Desert Animals*. New York: Crabtree Publishing, 1992. Children's book discussing endangered species found in the desert. Part of a series.

Wallace, M. *America's Deserts: Guide to Plants and Animals*. Golden, CO: Fulcrum Publishing, 1996. Children's book that focuses on the plants and animals found in North American deserts.

Williams, G. *Adaptation and Natural Selection*. Princeton, NJ: Princeton University Press, 1996. A detailed explanation of how natural selection works and the importance of adaptations for survival.

8. FILTERING WATER TO PREVENT POLUTION

Introduction

Would you drink tap water? For many people, the answer is no, because in some areas *contaminants* are suspected of seeping into the water that eventually comes through the tap. Whether or not the tap water in your area is safe to drink, we must all be *cognizant* of the need to keep contaminants not only out of drinking water but also out of our oceans, lakes, and rivers. For instance, warnings are painted on many storm drains to prevent dumping of garbage into drains, alerting people that garbage drains directly into the ocean. If garbage or *hazardous* wastes go down the storm drain, water habitats miles away may become *polluted*, negatively impacting animal and plant life in the area. In the United States, industry is thought to cause more than half the water pollution in the country and surrounding waters. In addition, hazardous *pollutants*, whether they come from industrial or domestic sources, can cause diseases ranging from liver and nerve damage to *dysentery*.

In this experiment, you will filter water and observe some of the pollutants that may be *contaminating* your water.

Time Needed

1 hour

What You Need

- large filtering tube (if not available, a glass funnel may be substituted)
- glass fish tank, medium-sized

- strainer, such as found in the kitchen
- charcoal pieces, 1/2 cup (about 118 milliliters [ml])
- sand, 1/2 cup (about 118 milliliters)
- gravel or small pebbles, 1/2 cup (about 118 ml)
- Micropore™ filter paper, 1 piece (available from a science supply company)
- coffee grounds, 1 cup (about 237 ml)
- measuring cup
- leaves, a handful
- scraps of paper
- 4 large beakers
- large glass bowl
- funnel
- long spoon or stick
- water, enough to fill the tank about halfway
- pen or pencil
- paper

Safety Precautions

Please review and follow the safety guidelines at the beginning of this volume.

What You Do

1. Fill the glass tank about halfway with water (Figure 1).

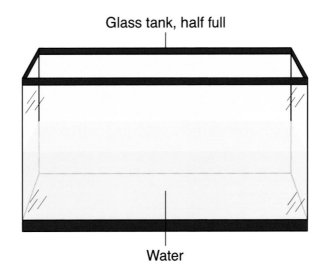

Glass tank, half full

Water

Figure 1

2. Add 1 cup (240 ml) of coffee grounds to the tank.

3. Add the scraps of paper to the tank.

4. Add a handful of leaves to the tank.

5. Stir the water to distribute the "pollutants" that you added.

6. Using one of the beakers, scoop up some of the now-dirty water.

7. First try screening the polluted water by pouring all of the water from the beaker through the strainer into a clean beaker (Figure 2).

Beaker

Strainer

Polluted water

Beaker

Strained water

Figure 2

8. Observe the difference between the water in the tank and the water in the beaker of strained water.

9. Record your observations.

10. Next, try sedimentation by allowing a beaker of polluted water to sit so that the pollutants can settle to the bottom of the beaker (Figure 3).

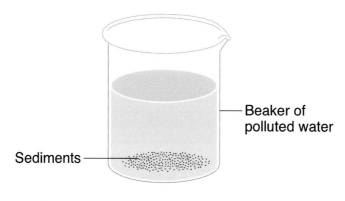

Beaker of polluted water

Sediments

Figure 3

11. Record your observations.

12. Fill the filtering tube or funnel with the following in this order: 1 layer of pebbles, 1 layer of sand, and 1 layer of charcoal (Figure 4).

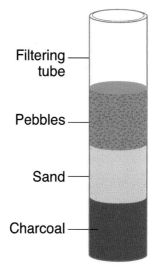

Filtering tube

Pebbles

Sand

Charcoal

Figure 4

13. Now attempt filtration by pouring the polluted water in the beaker that you just allowed to settle through the filtering tube into a clean beaker (Figure 5).

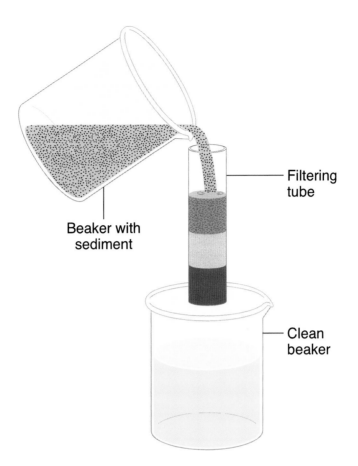

Figure 5

14. Observe the water in the beaker.

15. Record your observations.

16. Line the inside of the funnel with the filter paper (Figure 6).

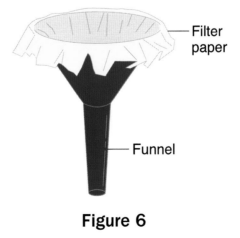

Figure 6

17. You will now perform the final filtration by pouring polluted water from the beaker through the funnel lined with filter paper into the last clean beaker (Figure 7).

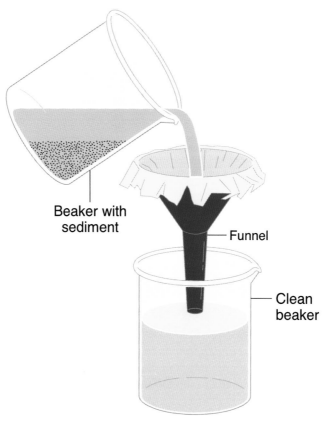

Beaker with sediment

Funnel

Clean beaker

Figure 7

18. Observe the water in the beaker.

19. Record your observations.

 **Observations**

1. Compare your observations after each step of the process. What was removed from the water at each step? How much cleaner did the water appear?

2. What additional step would you add to the filtration process if there were microorganisms in the water?

3. Why do we have to filter polluted water if we are not intending to drink it or use it ourselves?

Our Findings

Please refer to the Our Findings appendix at the back of this volume.

Further Reading

Donald, R. *Water Pollution*. Danbury, CT: Children's Press, 2002. Part of a series on the environment, a book for children about the dangers of water pollution.

Parks, P. *Water Pollution*. New York: Kidhaven Press, 2007. Part of a series on the environment for children, explains the problem of water pollution and ways to prevent it.

Shiva, V. *Water Wars: Privatization, Pollution, and Profit*. Brooklyn, NY: South End Press, 2002. Perspective of a scientist on the impact of privatization on the world population's access to clean water.

Vigil, K. *Clean Water: An Introduction to Water Quality and Pollution Control*. Corvallis, OR: Oregon State University Press, 2003. Provides information, not too technical, for concerned citizens about water quality.

"Water pollution." *The Columbia Encyclopedia*, 6th ed. 2008. Available online. URL: http://www.encyclopedia.com/doc/1E1-watrpollu.html. Accessed October 17, 2010. Entry on water pollution facts, dangers, sources, and legal implications.

"Water pollution." Environmental Protection Agency. Available online. URL: http://www.epa.gov/ebtpages/watewaterpollution.html. Accessed October 17, 2010. The official site of the EPA regarding the government's information about water pollution, its prevention, and treatment.

9. SUCCESSION: FOREST IN A JAR

Introduction

Succession is a process in which one *habitat* is *gradually* replaced by another habitat over time. *Ecological succession* is, therefore, the slow change of a *population* of *organisms* that occurs when the *environment* changes. These changes typically occur after a disturbance, such as a *volcanic eruption*, *drought*, fire, or *tsunami*. Succession may begin with an entirely new habitat, such as after a *lava flow* completely cools, or in an environment that has sustained major damage, such as a forest fire. If no soil is present when organisms first start to grow, the condition is known as *primary succession*; *secondary succession* occurs where there is already soil present. In the early stages of succession, *opportunistic species* usually survive and grow but are eventually taken over by more competitive species. Rain forests tend to hold many excellent examples of succession, as do areas that have experienced lava flows.

In this experiment, you will create a model forest in a jar and observe firsthand a form of succession.

Time Needed

30 minutes to prepare, a month or two to complete

What You Need

- soil, enough to fill the jar 2 in. (about 5 centimeters [cm])
- water, enough to fill the jar about 3 in. (about 7.6 cm) and additional water for keeping plants moist

✎   20 to 30 bird seeds

✎   4 sunflower seeds

✎   aquatic plant (can be purchased at an aquarium store)

✎   large glass jar

✎   paper

✎   pen or pencil

✎   a computer with Internet access or reference books

Safety Precautions

Please review and follow the safety guidelines at the beginning of this volume. Follow all Internet safety guidelines when using the computer.

What You Do

1. Add 2 in. (5 cm) of soil to the jar (Figure 1).

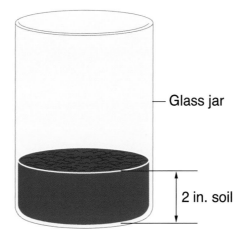

Glass jar

2 in. soil

2. Add about 3 in. (7.5 cm) of water to the jar.

3. Leaving the lid off, place the jar beside a window overnight.

4. The following day, plant the aquatic plant inside the jar (Figure 2).

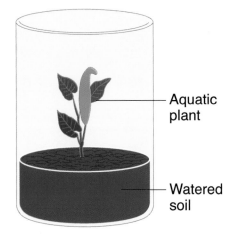

Figure 2

5. The water will slowly evaporate over time, but do not add more water. Record your observations.

6. Twice a week, add 3 or 4 bird seeds to the jar.

7. The seeds will most likely germinate and then eventually rot. Do not remove them from the jar. Record your observations.

8. Continue to add bird seeds once a week after the aquatic plant dies.

9. The bird seeds will now begin to grow. Record your observations.

10. At this point, add a few sunflower seeds. Record your observations.

11. Add water to the jar to keep the environment moist. The water represents the rainfall in a forest (Figure 3).

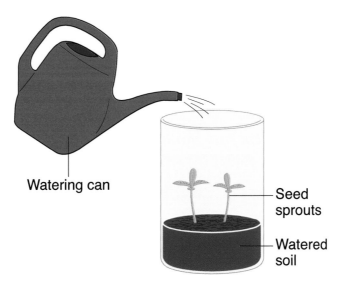

Figure 3

12. Record your observations.

 **Observations**

1. How is this different from a typical terrarium?
2. In what ways does this experiment model succession?
3. What conditions were needed for the bird seeds to grow?
4. What conditions were necessary for the sunflower seeds to grow?
5. Using a reference book or a computer with Internet access, research the process of succession in the rain forest, and create a poster illustrating the stages.

Our Findings

Please refer to the Our Findings appendix at the back of this volume.

Further Reading

Carson, R. *Mount St. Helens: The Eruption and Recovery of a Volcano*. Seattle: Sasquatch Books, 2002. An illustrated account of before and after the eruption.

———. *The Explosive Story of Mount St. Helens*. Green Forest, AR: Master Books, 2003. A pictorial overview of the eruption.

Dale, V., F. Swanson, and C. Crisafulli. *Ecological Responses to the 1980 Eruption of Mount St. Helens*. New York: Springer, 2005. Discusses the unique opportunity of observing succession after the eruption of a volcano in the United States.

"Frederic Edward Clements." *The Columbia Encyclopedia*, 6th ed. 2008. Available online. URL: http://www.encyclopedia.com/doc/1E1-Clements.html. Accessed September 29, 2009. A short encyclopedia entry about a pioneer in the study of succession.

Harper, Kristine. *The Mount St. Helens Volcanic Eruptions*. New York: Chelsea House, 2005. A straightforward narrative book on the events to the surrounding landscape.

"Mount Saint Helens." *The Columbia Encyclopedia*, 6th ed. 2008. Available online. URL: http://www.encyclopedia.com/doc/1E1-StHelensMt.html. Accessed September 29, 2010. Encyclopedia entry about Mount St. Helens and its eruption.

Walker, L., J. Walker, and R. Hobbs. *Linking Restoration and Ecological Succession*. New York: Springer, 2007. Technical book explaining disturbance ecology and invasion biology, among other topics related to succession.

10. DANDELION'S HABITAT

Introduction

A *habitat* is a place within the *environment* where an *organism* lives. There are many different types of environments and habitats, such as habitats found within *terrestrial* environments and marine environments. Different *ecosystems* combined with land *topography* and *climate* produce *distinct* habitats. Habitats are not strictly limited to an organism's "home." For an animal, a habitat must have food, water, and shelter, but might also include the area where it finds food. For plants, a habitat must have access to sunlight, water, soil, and nutrients. Very small organisms often live in *microhabitats*, while larger animals may occupy vast spaces. Often, plants or animals cannot thrive or survive outside of their habitats.

Humans live in habitats, too, which are not just the homes in which they live. The human habitat may also include where a person works, plays, or eats.

Scientists prefer to study organisms in their natural habitats. In this activity, you will observe a plant habitat. Specifically, you will study several areas to determine the preferred habitat of dandelions.

Time Needed

1 hour

What You Need

- ✐ yard stick (meterstick)
- ✐ pen or pencil

4 sticks

string, at least 2 yards (about 2 meters [m])

outdoor areas, some shady and some in direct sunlight, some with different types of soil

a computer with Internet access or a local library with reference books

Safety Precautions

Please review and follow the safety guidelines at the beginning of this volume. People with severe hay fever or other pollen- or plant-related allergies should take precautions to avoid exposure to allergens.

What You Do

1. Select an outdoor area.
2. Firmly drive a stick into the ground.
3. Measure about 20 in. (0.5 m) from the first stick, and drive the second stick in the ground there.
4. Repeat step 3 with 2 more sticks until you have a square area (Figure 1).

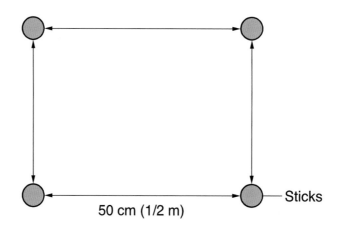

Figure 1

5. Tie one end of the string to one of the sticks.

6. Bring the string around the outside of each stick until you return to the first stick, creating an outline of a square (Figure 2). Tie the string to the first stick so that the string is pulled taught.

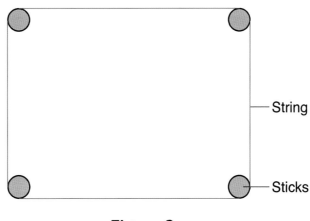

Figure 2

7. Observe and record your observations on the data table.

8. Untie the string and remove the sticks.

9. Repeat steps 1 to 8 three more times in other outdoor areas that receive different amounts of sunlight or shade or have different types of soil.

Data Table				
	Area 1	**Area 2**	**Area 3**	**Area 4**
Where is this area located?				
How much sunlight does the area receive?				

Data Table *(continued)*				
Describe the soil (sandy? clay? moist? dry?)				
Name other plants found in that area				
How many dandelions were in this area?				

 **Observations**

1. Which area had the most dandelions? What did this area have that the others did not?

2. Which area had the least dandelions? Why do you think the dandelions do not prefer that area?

3. What habitat do you think is best suited for dandelions?

4. Plants and animals prefer habitats where they can thrive. Select four of your favorite plants or animals and, using reference books or the Internet, research what types of habitats they prefer.

Our Findings

Please refer to the Our Findings appendix at the back of this volume.

Further Reading

"Dandelion." *The Columbia Encyclopedia*, 6th ed. 2008. Available online. URL: http://www.encyclopedia.com/doc/1E1-dandelio.html. Accessed September 23, 2010. Short article with details describing dandelions, facts about their seed dispersal, and their uses.

Dawson, J., and R. Lucas. *The Nature of Plants: Habitats, Challenges, and Adaptations*. Portland, OR: Timber Press, 2005. The author discusses the challenges that plants face to adapt to changes in their habitats.

"Endangered species." *The Columbia Encyclopedia*, 6th ed. 2008. Available online. URL: http://www.encyclopedia.com/doc/1E1-endanger.html. Accessed September 23, 2010. Article that explains how the human impact on animals habitats has led to the endangerment of many species.

Levy, J. *Discovering Mountains*. New York: PowerKids Press, 2007. Part of a series on world habitats, the author presents an overview of mountain organisms and their habitats.

Medina, S. *Graphing Habitats*. Portsmouth, NH: Heinemann, 2008. Teaches students how to create different types of graphs and data tables when studying habitats.

Schappert, P. *A World for Butterflies: Their Lives, Habitat and Future*. Ontario: Firefly Books, 2000. Well-illustrated book about butterflies and their environments.

11. SOIL MOISTURE AND PERMEABILITY

Introduction

For plants to grow, they must have access to water. Plants obtain their moisture from the soil, bringing it up from the soil through their roots. It is important that soil be able to hold the water plant roots need to absorb. However, some soil types hold more moisture than others. Loose, rich soil tends to hold more moisture; thick, claylike soil tends to resist absorption beneath the surface. The *composition* of the soil plays an important role in *permeability* and the soil's tendency to retain water. If the soil is unable to soak up or retain water, no moisture is available for the plant. Even when considering a plant in a flowerpot (i.e., not in the ground), take into account how well the pot retains water and how well it drains water.

In this experiment, you will use a simple method to compare and evaluate some basic characteristics of soil in relation to soil moisture and permeability.

Time Needed

1 hour

What You Need

- 3 glasses
- 1 cup sand
- 1 cup clay coil (about 236 milliliters [ml])
- 1 cup potting soil (about 236 ml)
- water, enough to fill 3 glasses

- 3 labels
- pen or pencil
- measuring cup
- paper, 1 sheet

Safety Precautions

Please review and follow the safety guidelines at the beginning of this volume.

What You Do

1. Label 1 glass "Sand."
2. Pour about 1 cup (240 cm^3) of sand into it.
3. Label the next glass "Clay."
4. Add about 1 cup (240 cm^3) of clay in the glass.
5. Label the third glass "Potting soil."
6. Add about 1 cup (240 cm^3) of potting soil in the glass.
7. You should now have 3 glasses lined up with 3 different types of soil (Figure 1).

Sand   Clay   Potting soil

Figure 1

8. Add water to each glass until the glasses are almost full (Figure 2).

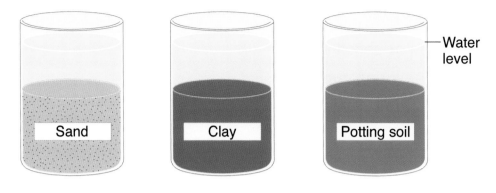

Figure 2

9. Observe what happens to the soil particles, and notice whether or not the particles settle back to the bottom quickly or remain suspended in the water.

10. Record your observations.

11. In the blank 3 glasses provided in Figure 3, draw a representation of what you observed regarding the water and the soil particles.

Figure 3

 Observations

1. Did the sand remain suspended in the water, sink to the bottom, or float? Why?

2. Did the clay remain suspended in the water, sink to the bottom, or float? Why?

3. Did the potting soil remain suspended in the water, sink to the bottom, or float? Why?

4. Based on your observations, which of the 3 types of soil would provide the best access for the roots of plants to be able to absorb water?

5. Why would the other 2 types of soil not be ideal for plant root systems to access moisture from the soil?

Our Findings

Please refer to the Our Findings appendix at the back of this volume.

Further Reading

Brickell, C. *American Horticultural Society A to Z Encyclopedia of Garden Plants*. New York: DK Adult, 2004. Comprehensive listing of all garden plants, an excellent basic reference.

Hancock, P., and B. Skinner. "Compaction and Consolidation of Soil." *The Oxford Companion to the Earth*. Oxford University Press, 2000. Available online. URL: http://www.encyclopedia. com/doc/10112-compactionandconsoldtnfsl.html. Accessed October 9, 2010. Short but detailed entry that explains how soil is consolidated, affecting the permeability of the soil.

Hillel, D. *Introduction to Environmental Soil Physics*. San Diego, CA: Academic Press, 2003. For advanced readers, explores the major topics of soil physics.

Ponte, K. *Retaining Soil Moisture in the American Southwest*. Santa Fe, NM: Sunstone Press, 2003. Provides information about the water in the dry southwestern area of the United States and what we must do to prevent using up all of those water resources.

"Root." *The Columbia Encyclopedia*, 6th ed. 2008. Accessed October 9, 2010. Available online. URL: http://www.encyclopedia.com/ doc/1E1-root1.html. Encyclopedia entry about the roots of plants, their structure, and their function.

Tompkins, P., and C. Bird. *The Secret Life of Plants*. New York: Harper Paperbacks, 1989. A spellbinding, fun book with practical scientific facts about plants.

12. CREATING A MODEL LANDFILL

Introduction

Most people have heard of the term "garbage dump." A dump typically refers to a *landfill*, where waste is *disposed*. Landfills may be temporary for short-term storage or permanent for burying trash. Because of the large amount of waste created by *consumers* each year, landfills are becoming increasingly full, and fewer communities are willing to have them nearby. In addition, the negative impact of landfills on many local communities has recently come to light. Some landfills have been known to contribute to water *pollution*, noise pollution, disease, and soil *contamination*. Also, some landfills were covered with soil and then used for developing housing. Typically, full areas of landfills are covered with soil and seeded for plant growth to prevent erosion of the top layers and the exposure of the trash beneath.

By using our *resources* more sparingly, not wasting, and *recycling*, we can reduce our use of landfills. However, some people find it difficult to imagine what happens to all the trash that is thrown away. After all, we toss it into a trashcan, and a waste disposal truck conveniently takes it away. Unfortunately, that trash does not disappear. It is most likely headed for a landfill.

In this activity, you will create a model landfill, *hypothesize* about product *decay*, and observe the results.

Time Needed

40 minutes to prepare, 35 to 40 days to complete

What You Need

- ✎ large, clear-plastic storage bin, at least 18 in. tall (about 46 cm), such as Rubbermaid® products
- ✎ soil, enough to fill the storage bin about 10 in. (29 cm) high
- ✎ aluminum foil, 12-by-12 in. (about 30-by-30 cm)
- ✎ apple, sliced
- ✎ 1 banana peel
- ✎ newspaper sheet, 12-by-12 in. (about 30-by-30 cm)
- ✎ 4 wooden sticks
- ✎ 4 labels
- ✎ tape
- ✎ grass seeds, small packet
- ✎ water, enough to water grass seeds
- ✎ ruler
- ✎ paper, 1 sheet
- ✎ pen or pencil

Safety Precautions

Please review and follow the safety guidelines at the beginning of this volume.

What You Do

1. Place about 4 in. (10 cm) of soil over the bottom of the storage bin.
2. Picture the bin as having 4 quadrants. You will be burying different items in each quadrant (Figure 1).

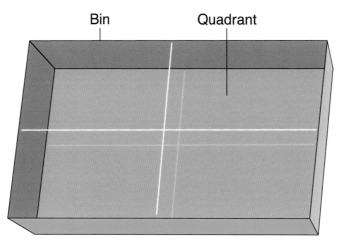

Figure 1

3. Add a few apple slices to one of the quadrants (Figure 2).

4. Add some pieces of the banana peel to another quadrant (Figure 2).

5. Tear up the aluminum foil into 3 or 4 pieces, and add those to another quadrant (Figure 2).

6. Tear up the newspaper into 3 or 4 pieces and add those to another quadrant (Figure 2).

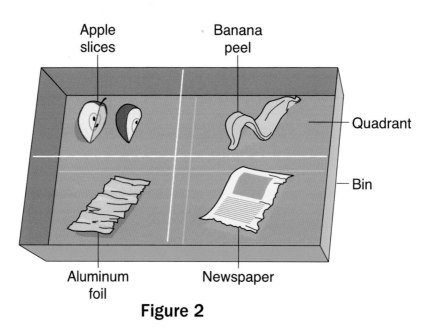

Figure 2

7. Cover the items with the remaining soil.

8. Place wooden sticks in each of the 4 quadrants.

9. Attach labels to each of the sticks with the name of the item buried in that quadrant (Figure 3).

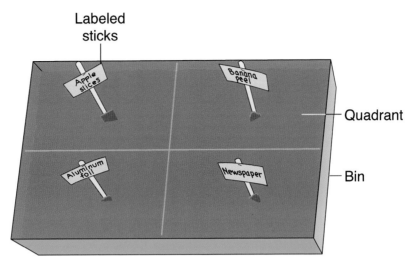

Figure 3

10. Hypothesize about the extent to which each of the items you buried will decay.

11. Record your hypotheses.

12. Dig up your items after 10 days.

13. Record your observations about any decay.

14. Rebury the items.

15. Repeat steps 12 to 14 two more times.

16. After the third check on day 30, add grass seeds to the soil.

17. Water the soil often enough to help the grass seeds grow.

 **Observations**

1. What was your original hypothesis about the possible rate of decay of each item?

   a. apple slices

   b. bananas

      c. aluminum foil

      d. newspaper

2. Were your hypotheses correct? What observations support your answers to these questions?

3. What purpose do plants serve over a landfill?

4. How did this activity impact your opinions on recycling, landfills, and the large amount of garbage produced annually?

Our Findings

Please refer to the Our Findings appendix at the back of this volume.

Further Reading

"Landfills." The United States Environmental Protection Agency. 2009. Available online. URL: http://www.epa.gov/waste/nonhaz/municipal/landfill.htm. Accessed October 1, 2010. Official information about landfills from the U.S. government.

Melosi, M. *Garbage in the Cities: Refuse Reform and the Environment*. Pittsburgh: University of Pittsburgh Press, 2004. Overview of how garbage disposal came into existence and its current impact.

Newman, W., and W. Holton. *Boston's Back Bay: The Story of America's Greatest Nineteenth-Century Landfill Project*. Boston: Northeastern, 2007. Historical background on an area that is now home to expensive houses but was once a polluted marsh.

"OC Waste and Recycling." *OCgov.com*. 2009. Available online. URL: http://egov.ocgov.com/ocgov/Info%20OC/Departments%20&%20Agencies/OC%20Waste%20&%20Recycling/Landfill%20Information. Accessed October 1, 2010. Information and procedures about landfills in Orange County, California.

"Sunshine Canyon Landfill." North Valley Coalition. 2008. Available online. URL: http://www.nodump.com/. Accessed October 1, 2010. Documents a community's efforts to shut down a major landfill serving Los Angeles and the politics involved.

Tammemagi, H. *The Waste Crisis: Landfills, Incinerators, and the Search for a Sustainable Future*. Oxford: Oxford University Press, 1999. Explores the realities and politics of dumping trash in landfills.

13. INVESTIGATING ALTERNATIVE FUELS

Introduction

The burning of *fuels* produces many *pollutants*. Most pollutants of this nature are either a *gas* or a *solid*; the gaseous pollutants in the air include *sulfur dioxide*, *carbon monoxide*, *carbon dioxide*, *nitrogen oxides*, and *ozone*; the solid pollutants include lead and various *particulate* matter. It takes only a small amount of these gases and solids to pollute the air. Pollution causes *acid rain*, contributes to *global warming*, creates breathing problems, harms trees, and causes certain diseases. Automobiles are a large source of pollution due to the burning of *fossil fuels*. Fossil fuels not only damage the air; they also are a *non-renewable resource*. Scientists are working *diligently* to find *alternative* fuels that are not as harmful to the Earth.

In this experiment, you will observe the particulate matter caused by automobiles; you will also research alternative fuels.

Time Needed

3 to 4 hours

What You Need

- ✎ scissors
- ✎ 6 coffee filters
- ✎ 6 index cards, 3 in. by 5 in. (about 8 x 13 cm)
- ✎ magnifying glass
- ✎ access to at least 6 automobiles and trucks, a variety of old and new vehicles, large and small

✎   pen or pencil

✎   ruler

✎   glue stick

✎   paper, 1 sheet

✎   computer with Internet access

Safety Precautions

Please review and follow the safety guidelines at the beginning of this volume. Get permission from vehicle owners prior to testing. Do not touch the tailpipe. Avoid breathing fumes. Conduct the experiment in a well-ventilated area. Adult supervision is recommended. Follow all computer safety guidelines.

What You Do

1. Cut the coffee filters into 6 rectangles 2 in. (5 cm) by 4 in. (10 cm) long (Figure 1).

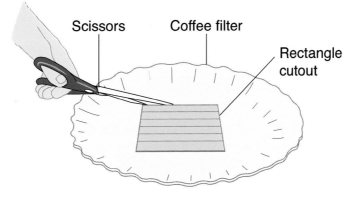

Figure 1

2. Glue each rectangular piece of coffee filter to a separate index card (Figure 2).

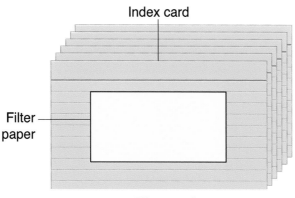

Figure 2

3. Have the owner of one vehicle start the engine. Important: Make sure the car is in "park" and the emergency brake is engaged.

4. Write the name of the make and model of the vehicle on the back of the index card.

5. Hold the index card about 6 in. (15 cm) away from the exhaust pipe for 1 minute (Figure 3). Be careful not to touch the exhaust pipe as it will get very hot! Do not breathe in the fumes.

Figure 3

6. Ask the owner to turn off the car engine.

7. Repeat steps 3 to 6 with five other vehicles, using a fresh index card and filter paper for each.

8. Place the index cards near each other, and inspect them under the magnifying glass.

9. Estimate the number of particulates per square inch (6.25 cm^2) on each piece of filter paper.

10. Complete the data table.

11. Using a computer with Internet access, research alternative fuels that do not pollute the environment. Write a paragraph describing one fuel that you believe is "Earth friendly" and could be used as an alternative to a fossil fuel.

Data Table			
Make and model of car	Older or newer car?	Estimated number of particulates per square inch	Other observations

 **Observations**

1. Which car had the most particulates per square inch? Was that car older or newer? Large or small?

2. What did you observe on the filter papers that made it obvious there were pollutants in the exhaust?

3. How do you think these pollutants affect you and other organisms?

4. Which alternative fuel did you research? What about it makes it a better alternative to fossil fuel?

Our Findings

Please refer to the Our Findings appendix at the back of this volume.

Further Reading

Gibilisco, S. *Alternative Energy Demystified*. New York: McGraw-Hill Professional, 2006. Explains in detail how alternative energy sources work, such as hybrid cars and solar energy.

"Global warming." *The Columbia Encyclopedia*, 6th ed. 2008. Available online. URL: http://www.encyclopedia.com/doc/1E1-globalwa.html. Accessed October 10, 2010. Encyclopedia entry about global warming, its causes and effects.

"Global warming search results." The United States Environmental Protection Agency. 2009. Available online. URL: http://nlquery. epa.gov/epasearch/epasearch?areaname=&areacontacts =http%3A%2F%2Fwww.epa.gov%2Fepahome%2Fcomments. htm&areasearchurl=&result_template=epafiles_default.xsl&action=fil tersearch&filter=&typeofsearch=epa&querytext=global+warming&GO =SEARCH. Accessed October 10, 2010. Provides links to up-to-date EPA articles on the topic of global warming.

Miller, K. *What If We Run Out of Fossil Fuels*. Danbury, CT: Children's Press, 2002. Children's book with many facts about fossil fuels and scenarios about what might happen if we run out or continue to use them excessively.

Morris, N. *Fossil Fuels (Energy Source)*. London: Franklin Watts, 2008. A look at different energy sources and how their power is used.

14. DETERMINING SOIL QUALITY

Introduction

When it comes to supporting the growth of plants, not all soils are the same. Soil *composition* can either help or *impede* plant growth. Plants may *thrive* in various types of soil but not be able to grow at all in others. Soil type refers to soil *texture*, based on the size of finely ground rocks composing the soil. This includes sand, *silt*, and clay. Different types of "dirt" can also contain varying amounts of *nutrients*, while other soils might have had all of their nutrients already *leached*. Some of these *vital* nutrients include *nitrogen*, *phosphorous*, and *potassium*. Spaces between soil particles can also affect the soil's ability to hold water, which is essential for plant growth. Extremes in temperature can affect the survival of plants. Also, plants require access to sunlight and *carbon dioxide* so that *photosynthesis* can take place.

In this experiment, you will test the quality of soil by comparing the amount of plant growth in different types of soil.

Time Needed

45 minutes to prepare, 3 weeks to complete

What You Need

- potting soil, a few cups
- yard soil, hard and compacted, a few cups

- yard soil, loose and fluffy, a few cups
- 3 small flowerpots
- 3 saucers to go under the flowerpots
- water, enough for daily watering of plants
- 9 bean seeds
- 3 small wooden stakes or sticks
- ruler
- trowel
- paper, 1 sheet
- pen or pencil
- graph paper, 1 sheet
- 3 labels (or masking tape)
- black permanent marker
- colored pencils

Safety Precautions

Please review and follow the safety guidelines at the beginning of this volume.

What You Do

1. Fill 1 flowerpot with potting soil.
2. Label the pot "potting soil" (Figure 1).

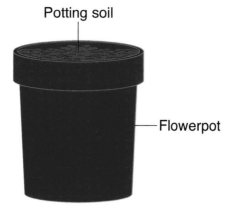

Figure 1

3. Fill the next pot with compacted yard soil and label it accordingly.

4. Fill the final pot with the loose yard soil and label it accordingly.

5. Place all 3 pots on the saucers.

6. Add enough water to each of the pots to moisten the soil.

7. Plant 3 bean seeds, spaced slightly apart from each other, into each of the 3 pots (Figure 2).

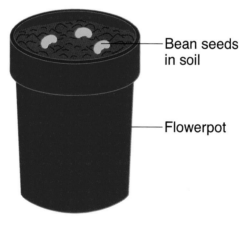

Figure 2

8. Insert a stake into each of the 3 pots so that the bean plants will be able to "climb" as they grow, making it easier to measure their height.

9. Place all 3 pots outside in a sunny area where you can easily check on them.

10. On the data table, record the date on which you planted the seeds.

11. Water the pots daily, keeping the soil moist but not soggy.

12. When you notice that any of the seeds have sprouted, record on the data table the pots in which they grew and the date.

13. Every few days over the next 3 weeks, measure the height of the bean sprouts.

14. Record your results on the data table.

Data Table								
Planted on Date:								
Potting soil								
Compacted soil								
Loose soil								

 **Observations**

1. Which soil held the seeds that sprouted first? Which soil held the seeds that sprouted last?

2. Which soil held the seeds that grew the tallest? Which soil held the seeds that grew the least?

3. Using the graph paper and colored pencils, make a graph showing the growth of the plants in each pot over time.

4. Based on your observations, which of the pots held the highest-quality soil? Explain.

5. Why may this information be useful to farmers?

Our Findings

Please refer to the Our Findings appendix at the back of this volume.

Further Reading

"Crop rotation." *A Dictionary of World History*. 2000. Available online. URL: http://www.encyclopedia.com/doc/1048-croprotation.html. Accessed September 24, 2010. Encyclopedia-like entry about the benefits of rotating crops.

Jeavons, J. *How to Grow More Vegetables and Fruits Than You Ever Thought Possible in Less Land Than You Can Imagine*. Berkley, CA: Ten Speed Press, 2006. Essential reference on sustainable gardening.

Kohnke, H., and D. P. Franzmeier. *Soil Science Simplified*. Prospect Heights, IL: Waveland Press, 1941. Overview of the principles and concepts related to soil quality, including tables and charts.

Smith, D. "Swap Beans for Corn?" *Farm Journal*, 128 (3), pp. 15–16, February 1, 2004. Explains the profits and benefits of rotating soybean crops with corn crops rather than just growing corn.

Stell, E. *Secrets to Great Soil*. North Adams, MA: Storey Publishing, 1998. Practical and technical look at soil nutrients, including gardening tips.

U.S. Geological Survey. Available online. URL: http://www.usgs.gov/. Accessed September 24, 2010. The United States government's site for public information related to Earth's resources and natural hazards.

15. GROWING PLANTS WITHOUT SOIL

Introduction

Soil contains *nutrients* and oxygen absorbed by the *roots* of plants, as well as water that is essential for plant life. However, plants can grow without the presence of soil. This is not a concept we first teach a child when explaining how to grow plants with a pot full of soil and some seeds. The truth is, some plants do grow naturally without soil, for example *epiphytes*. Epiphytes are plants that grow on other plants such as certain *orchids*. Some seeds sprout in the absence of soil (but need water) because the seeds contain enough nutrients to allow them to sprout. Even plants that typically require soil for growth may be grown without soil if the plant supplied with the water, nutrients, and support needed for growth and life processes. Many growers use *hydroponics* to grow plants without the presence of soil. Instead, the roots are soaked in a nutrient solution, and artificial means are used to support the plants' stems. Hydroponics can be used when there is not enough land available for growing plants, especially plants that are a source of food.

In this experiment, you will grow a plant without the benefit of soil.

Time Needed

1 hour

What You Need

- 4 toothpicks
- sweet potato

- glass
- water, enough to fill the glass most of the way
- pen or pencil
- paper
- cotton ball, about 2 dozen
- 8 lima beans
- plastic plate
- clear plastic wrap, enough to wrap around the plate

Safety Precautions

Please review and follow the safety guidelines at the beginning of this volume.

What You Do

1. Fill the glass about three-quarters with water.
2. Place toothpicks at about equal intervals around the circumference of the sweet potato, as close to the middle of the potato as possible (Figure 1).

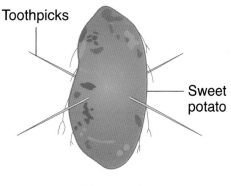

Toothpicks

Sweet potato

Figure 1

3. Position the sweet potato in the glass so that the toothpicks rest on top of the glass (Figure 2).

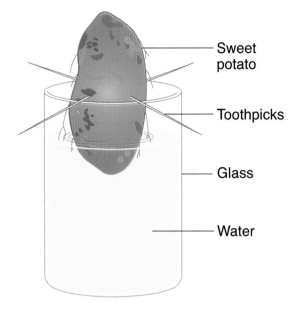

Figure 2

4. Place the jar near a window that gets sunlight.

5. Moisten the cotton balls and place them on the plastic plate.

6. Put the lima beans on top of the moistened cotton balls, with space between them (Figure 3).

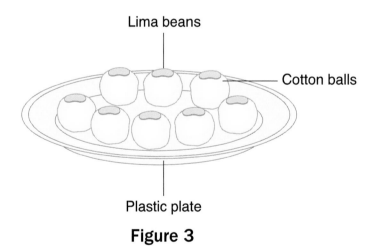

Figure 3

7. Cover the plate completely in clear plastic wrap, and tape the wrap in place. Make sure that the plastic wrap is tight against the lima beans and cotton balls.

8. Poke 4 or 5 small holes in the plastic wrap.

9. Carefully lift the plate upright and place it against the window so that the lima beans are facing out the window (Figure 4). Tape the plate in place so it cannot fall.

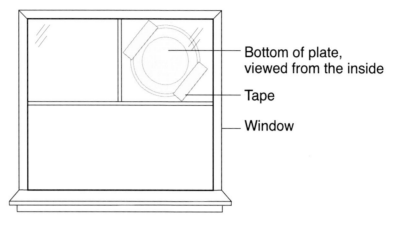

Figure 4

10. After 7 days, remove the plate from the window and the sweet potato from the windowsill.
11. Record your observations of the lima beans and the sweet potato.

 **Observations**

1. What happened to the sweet potato? How was the plant able to grow?
2. What happened to the lima beans? How did this happen?
3. If you want to continue growing your plants, why must they now be planted in soil?
4. When may it be useful to grow plants without soil?

Our Findings

Please refer to the Our Findings appendix at the back of this volume.

Further Reading

"Epiphyte." *The Columbia Encyclopedia*, 6th ed. 2008. Available online. URL: http://www.encyclopedia.com/doc/1E1-epiphyte.html. Accessed October 10, 2010. Short entry explaining what an epiphyte is and providing a few examples.

"Hydroponics." *The Columbia Encyclopedia*, 6th ed. 2008. Available online. URL: http://www.encyclopedia.com/doc/1E1-hydropon. html. Accessed October 10, 2010. Short entry that explains how hydroponics works, including what types of physical support are provided for the plants.

Kenyon, S. *Hydroponics for the Home Gardener*. Ontario: Key Porter Books, 2005. Easy-to-follow instructions for growing organic foods without soil.

Resh, H. *Hobby Hydroponics*. Boca Raton, FL: CRC, 2003. Explains the concept of hydroponics to the layman, with a brief history of the process.

Roberto, K. *How-To Hydroponics*, 4th ed. New York: Futuregarden, 2003. Provides step-by-step guides and photographs for your own hydroponics garden.

"What Is Hydroponics?" 2008. Available online. URL: http://www.simplyhydro.com/whatis.htm. Accessed October 10, 2010. Describes in detail the mechanism and value of hydroponics.

16. TESTING AND COMPARING WATER QUALITY

Introduction

You can go to the kitchen sink, turn on the faucet, and water comes out. But do you drink that water? Some people believe there are *toxins* or *contaminants* in their tap water that make it unhealthy to drink, while others say this is nonsense. However, the bottled-water industry is a booming business in this country. Is bottled water any safer to drink that the tap water from your kitchen sink? There are many contaminants that can make their way into our water sources, while other *substances* are added to our water to purify it. Contaminants may even come from water pipes at home. Some of the substances you may find in water include *sediments*, lead, iron, copper, *nitrates*, *nitrites*, *chlorine*, *chloramine*, and *bacteria*. Many of these contaminants can cause serious diseases or even death.

In this experiment, you will test the water purity of different water samples, research the contaminants, and determine if any exceed acceptable levels.

Time Needed

2 hours to begin, a few days to complete

What You Need

- water, at least 1 cup (about 236 ml), from at least each of 4 different sources (e.g., your kitchen tap, bathroom tap, water fountain at the park or at school, bottled water)

- 4 water test kits (available at hardware stores and from science supply companies)

- ✎ lined paper, a few sheets
- ✎ pen or pencil
- ✎ 4 clean, clear, unused plastic cups
- ✎ 4 labels
- ✎ black marker
- ✎ computer with Internet access or access to science reference books in a library

Safety Precautions

Please review and follow the safety guidelines at the beginning of this volume. Adult supervision is recommended when accessing the Internet. Follow all computer safety guidelines.

What You Do

1. Collect water from your kitchen tap in a plastic cup.
2. Label the cup "Kitchen sink" (Figure 1).

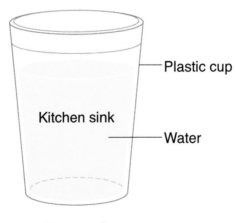

Figure 1

3. Repeat steps 1 and 2 for each of the following and label them accordingly: water from your bathroom sink, water from a water fountain, and bottled water.

4. Allow the water in each cup to settle. Observe for sediments (Figure 2).

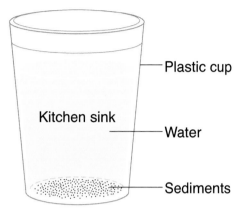

Figure 2

5. Record your observations.

6. Using the test kits, test each of the water samples for the following:

   a. lead   f. iron

   b. nitrates   g. chloramine

   c. nitrites   h. copper

   d. chlorine   i. bacteria

   e. sodium   j. pH

   Note that for some test kits, you will need to mail in your tests; then the results will be mailed back to you.

7. Using reference sources, research each of the items you tested to determine what their "acceptable" levels are and whether or not each sample contained acceptable or unhealthy levels of each. It is recommended you visit this Web site http://www.epa.gov.

Data Table								
Sediments	Kitchen tap water		Bathroom tap water		Water fountain		Bottled water	
	Amount	Safe?	Amount	Safe?	Amount	Safe?	Amount	Safe?
Lead								
Nitrates								
Nitrites								
Chlorine								
Sodium								
Iron								
Chloramines								
Copper								
Bacteria								
pH								

 **Observations**

1. Did any of your samples contain unhealthy amounts of any of the substances? If so, which ones?

2. Did any of your samples pass with acceptable levels of all substances? If so, which ones?

3. Will the results of this experiment influence your choice of drinking water?

4. Why do you think the United States Environmental Protection Agency must set limits on these substances?

Our Findings

Please refer to the Our Findings appendix at the back of this volume.

Further Reading

Ingram, C. *The Drinking Water Book: How to Eliminate Harmful Toxins From Your Water*. Berkeley, CA: Celestial Arts, 2006. Explains in laymen's terms the contaminants found in drinking water and how to reduce your intake of them.

Morris, R. *The Blue Death: The Intriguing Past and Present Danger of the Water You Drink*. New York: Harper Paperbacks, 2008. Told by a physician, a public health expert, the book reviews the pathogens found in drinking water and the diseases they cause.

Royte, E. *Bottlemania: Big Business, Local Springs, and the Battle Over America's Drinking Water*. London: Bloomsbury, 2009. The author explains that most tap water is safe to drink, yet the bottled-water business is booming in America due to fears of contaminants.

"Search results." 2009. United States Environmental Protection Agency. Available online. URL: http://nlquery.epa.gov/epasearch/ epasearch?areaname=&areacontacts=http%3A%2F%2Fwww.epa. gov%2Fepahome%2Fcomments.htm&areasearchurl=&result_ template=epafiles_default.xsl&action=filtersearch&filter=&typeofsearc h=epa&querytext=drinking+water&GO=SEARCH. Accessed October 22, 2010. Links to the EPA's resources and information on drinking water.

"A Visit to a Wastewater-Treatment Plant: Primary Treatment of Wastewater." 2009. United States Geological Survey. Available online. URL: http://ga.water.usgs.gov/edu/wwvisit.html. Accessed October 22, 2010. About the protection of public health by treating waste water.

Zaslow, S., and G. Herman. 1996. "Health Effects of Drinking Water Contaminants." http://www.bae.ncsu.edu/programs/extension/publicat/wqwm/he393.html. Accessed October 22, 2010. Describes illness resulting from drinking contaminated water.

17. MATCHING ANIMALS TO THEIR BIOMES

Introduction

Biomes are biological *communities* that contain similar *climate*, *vegetation*, and other *factors*. The *physical environment* of a biome includes its *precipitation* levels and temperature. In water, biomes may include the *salinity* and depth of the water. *Terrestrial* biomes are those located on land and include the *tundra*, *taiga*, *temperate coniferous forest*, *deciduous forest*, *rain forest*, *grasslands (savannah)*, and *deserts*. Water biomes are divided into *marine* biomes and *freshwater* biomes depending on the salinity of the water. Marine biomes are characterized by their depth and include oceans, coral *reefs*, and *estuaries*. Freshwater biomes are also characterized by depth, but in addition they are characterized by whether the water is still or moving. Examples of Freshwater biomes include lakes, streams, rivers, ponds, and *wetlands*.

In this activity, you will research biomes and the animals you find in them. You will also graph your results and compare and contrast two of the biomes you study.

Time Needed

about 4 to 5 hours

What You Need

- ✎ white paper, 1 sheet
- ✎ pen or pencil
- ✎ colored pencils, crayons, or markers

- box of animal crackers
- graph paper, 2 sheets
- access to reference books or a computer with Internet access.

Safety Precautions

Please review and follow the safety guidelines at the beginning of this volume. Follow all safety guidelines for Internet use.

What You Do

1. Fold the sheet of paper once, lengthwise (Figure 1).

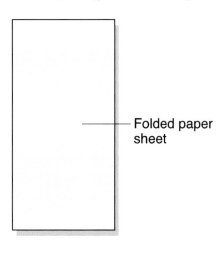

Folded paper sheet

Figure 1

2. Without unfolding the paper, fold it again into thirds crosswise (Figure 2).

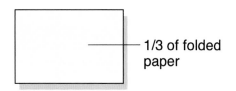

1/3 of folded paper

Figure 2

3. Open up the paper. You should have 6 spaces defined by the folds (Figure 3).

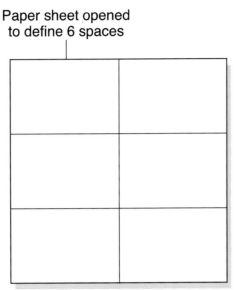

Paper sheet opened
to define 6 spaces

Figure 3

4. Write the following biome names into the spaces, one in each space (Figure 4): Tundra, Deciduous forest, Grassland, Rain forest, Desert, and Ocean. Do not print with big letters as you will be drawing in and adding to the spaces.

Tundra	Deciduous forest
Grassland	Rain forest
Desert	Ocean

Figure 4

5. Using reference books or the Internet, look up the six biomes and find pictures of them.

6. Draw a picture of each biome in the matching space on your paper.

7. Open the box of animal crackers.

8. Place each animal cracker on the space with the biome in which the animal is most likely to live based on your research. Consider what type of animal it is: for example, if it is a bear, designate it as a brown bear or a polar bear.

9. Complete the data table.

Data Table				
Biome	Animal	Number of this animal in paper space	Animal	Number of this animal in paper space
Tundra				
Deciduous forest				
Grassland				
Rain forest				
Desert				
Ocean				

Data Table *(continued)*				
Biome	**Animal**	**Number of this animal in paper space**	**Animal**	**Number of this animal in paper space**
Tundra				
Deciduous forest				
Grassland				
Rain forest				
Desert				
Ocean				

 Observations

1. Was it difficult to determine in which biome the animal lived? Why?

2. Using a sheet of graph paper, make a graph of how many of each animal was found in the space. Which animals were most abundant? Which were least abundant?

3. Make another graph of how many types of animals were placed in each biome. Which biomes had the most different types of animals? Which ones had the least?

4. Select two of the biomes and create a Venn diagram showing the similarities and differences of the two biomes, including the types of animals that live there. A Venn diagram should be set up as in Figure 5:

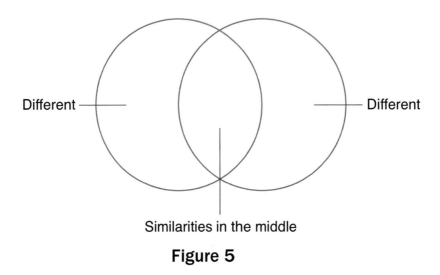

Figure 5

Our Findings

Please refer to the Our Findings appendix at the back of this volume.

Further Reading

Davis, B. *Biomes and Ecosystems*. New York: Gareth Stevens Publishing, 2007. Children's book that includes photographs of the biomes and their animals; includes new vocabulary terms.

McGinley, M. *Encyclopedia of Earth*. "Biome." 2008. Available online. URL: http://www.eoearth.org/article/Biome. Accessed October 9, 2010. Detailed explanation of a biome, along with links to further information on the specific types of biomes.

Moore, Peter D. *Tundra*. New York: Chelsea House, 2006. Profusely illustrated with color photographs and line art, this is a clearly written book on the geography, geology, ecology, and future of the biome.

Ritter, Michael E. *The Physical Environment: An Introduction to Physical Geography*. 2006. Available online. URL: http://www.uwsp. edu/geo/faculty/ritter/geog101/textbook/title_page.html). Accessed October 9, 2010. Detailed information about each biome, where they are found in the world, their climates, their vegetation, and their animal life.

Tagliaferro, L. *Explore the Tropical Rain Forest*. Mankato, MN: Capstone Press, 2007. Children's book that is colorful and covers the topic of the biome of the rain forest.

————. *Explore the Tundra*. Mankato, MN: Capstone Press, 2008. Children's book with simple sentences that discusses the biome known as the tundra.

Woodward, S. *Biomes of Earth: Terrestrial, Aquatic, and Human Dominated*. Westport, CT: Greenwood Press, 2003. A book for high-level readers that thoroughly lays the groundwork for understanding the different types of biomes.

18. CREATING A LIVING BIOME

Introduction

Biomes are areas with similar *climates* that contain *communities* of *organisms*. Because of this characteristic, biomes found in different parts of the world may contain similar types of organisms because the *environmental* conditions are similar. The climate of the biome is generally influenced by *geography* and is primarily a result of the average annual temperature and *precipitation*. Some areas may be drier than others, depending on whether they receive high or low levels of precipitation. The plants and animals within those biomes have *evolved* to *adapt* to their *environments*, with ability to live with high heat, freezing temperatures, or low humidity. For instance, the desert is a biome where plants such as the cactus have adapted to store water, reduce water loss, and open their *stomata* at night.

In this activity, you will create two live models of biomes—a mini-biome and a tropical biome complete with animals.

Time Needed
1 to 3 hours to prepare, 2 to 4 weeks to complete

What You Need

Mini-biome

- empty 2-liter soda bottle
- scissors
- gallon-size clear Ziploc® bag
- pebbles, enough to fill the bottom of the bottle 1 in.

- potting soil, about 2 cups (about 472 ml)
- grass seeds
- bean seeds
- water, enough to wet the soil
- ruler
- lined paper, a few sheets
- pen or pencil

Advanced biome

- fish tank with screen cover
- light source for tank (available at aquarium or reptile stores)
- heat source for tank (available at aquarium or reptile stores)
- small, shallow bowl
- gravel, enough to cover the bottom of the tank
- soil, about the same amount of the gravel plus an additional 8 cups
- tablespoon
- thermometer
- vinegar, 1/2 cup (about 118 ml)
- running water
- 4 small flowerpots
- 2 tropical ferns (available from a nursery)
- 2 philodendrons (available from a nursery)
- house gecko (available at an aquarium or pet store)
- gecko pet book or instructions for care (available from a pet store or a book store)
- crickets (to feed the gecko)
- mealworms (to feed the gecko)

Safety Precautions

Please review and follow the safety guidelines at the beginning of this volume. Adult supervision is recommended. Always obtain parental permission before buying or bringing home an animal and insects. Always wash your hands before and after handling animals and insects. Handle animals with care. Follow animal care instructions provided by the pet store. Keep in mind that animals require constant care.

What You Do

Mini-biome

1. Cut the soda bottle in half crosswise, and keep the bottom of the container (Figure 1).

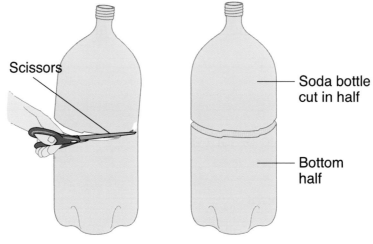

Scissors

Soda bottle cut in half

Bottom half

Figure 1

2. Add the pebbles to the empty bottom half of the container so that they are about 1/2 in. (1.25 cm) deep (Figure 2).

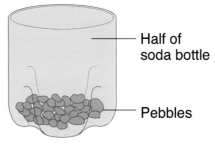

Half of soda bottle

Pebbles

Figure 2

3. Add about 1 1/2 cups (360 cm^3) of potting soil over the pebbles.

4. Sprinkle the seeds over the soil.

5. Add the remaining soil over the seeds (Figure 3).

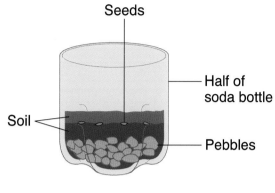

Seeds

Half of
soda bottle

Soil

Pebbles

Figure 3

6. Pour water on the soil until the soil is moistened and water is pooling around the pebbles.

7. Place the container into the Ziploc® bag, upright, being careful not to tip it over (Figure 4).

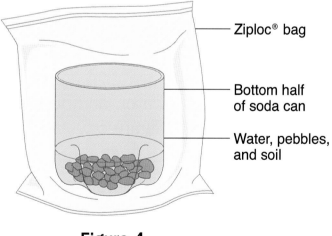

Ziploc® bag

Bottom half
of soda can

Water, pebbles,
and soil

Figure 4

8. Seal the bag. You now have a mini-biome.

9. Observe your biome over the next 2 weeks and record your observations.

Advanced biome

10. Add the vinegar to the fish tank.

11. Run water into the fish tank to make a weak vinegar/water solution to clean the tank. (Never use detergents; they can harm living organisms in a tank.)

12. Rinse the tank thoroughly with clean water so that no vinegar remains.

13. Line the bottom of the tank with gravel.

14. Add a layer of soil over the gravel (Figure 5).

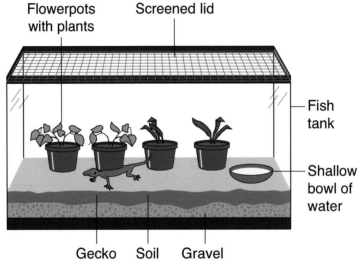

Figure 5

15. Fill the small bowl with water, and put it off to one side of the tank on top of the soil (Figure 5).

16. Add soil to the flowerpots to fill them 2/3 full.

17. Plant the ferns and philodendrons into the small flowerpots.

18. Place the flowerpots into your tank (Figure 5).

19. Set the lighting and heating sources for the gecko according to the information in the pet instructions.

20. Gently place the gecko into the biome (Figure 5).

21. Secure the screened lid over the tank so the gecko cannot get out.

22. Add cricket and/or mealworms to the tank according to the feeding schedule in the pet instructions.

23. Add water to the bowl every day or two so that the gecko has plenty of water.

 **Observations**

1. How is the mini-biome able to remain closed yet the plants grow and have water?

2. Why were tropical plants added to the more-advanced living model biome?

3. What other model biomes could you create in a tank or in your yard? What materials would they require?

Our Findings

Please refer to the Our Findings appendix at the back of this volume.

Further Reading

Allaby, Michael. *Tropical Forests*. New York: Chelsea House, 2006. A profusely illustrated reference that is ideal for students researching topics related to tropical forests.

Bartlett, R. D., and P. Bartlett. *Geckos (Complete Owner's Manual)*. New York: Barron's Educational Series, 2006. Expert advice on everyday care, health, feeding, and housing geckos.

Beehler, B. *Lost Worlds: Adventures in the Tropical Rainforest*. New Haven, CT: Yale University Press, 2009. Discusses the rain forests and their importance to the world.

"Climate." *The Columbia Encyclopedia*, 6th ed. 2008. Available online. URL: http://www.encyclopedia.com/doc/1E1-climate.html. Accessed October 23, 2010. Detailed entry about what determines climate and how it is defined.

Hewitt, T. *Complete Book of Cacti and Succulents*. New York: DK Adult, 1997. History and cultivation of cacti, accompanied by informative color photographs.

Morgan, B. *Rainforest*. New York: DK Adult, 2006. Beautiful color photographs of tropical rain forests.

"Tropical Rainforest Information Center." Michigan State University, 2009. Available online. URL: http://www.trfic.msu.edu/. Accessed October 23, 2010. A comprehensive Web site developed in conjunction with NASA that provides information, maps, and other materials regarding tropical rain forests.

19. STUDYING A FRESHWATER HABITAT

Introduction

Habitats vary widely and are found even in the most unlikely places. A common, overlooked habitat is the freshwater habitat, which can be found in ponds, streams, creeks, rivers, and other sources of water. Freshwater habitats can occur anywhere there is fresh water flowing or collecting. It is even possible to have a freshwater habitat on your lawn if there is an area that collects water for large periods of time. Eventually, organisms grow there, ranging from plant life to insect *larvae*. However, these habitats can be *fragile*. Changes to the water caused by *pollution* can negatively impact the *organisms* living there. Such changes in water quality typically lead to some organisms dying and others thriving, unless the *pollutants* are so *hazardous* and widespread as to kill all life in the area. As water quality *deteriorates*, different species will be found in that habitat.

In this activity, you will visit a local freshwater habitat, study the organisms that live there, and attempt to identify them.

Time Needed

2 hours

What You Need

- field guide to pond life, available from a library or bookstore
- small fishnet
- larger net with small mesh
- long-handled dip net

- collecting bucket, white
- pH paper
- thermometer
- meterstick or tape measure
- ruler
- stopwatch
- magnifying glass
- fish float or a light object that can float on water, such as a leaf
- old boots
- composition or sketchbook
- pencil

Safety Precautions

Please review and follow the safety guidelines at the beginning of this volume. Be cautious when walking or standing on slippery surfaces. Adult supervision is highly recommended.

What You Do

1. Find the freshwater habitat closest to you, such as a local pond or creek. If no such habitat exists near you, a drainage ditch with water may be used as a substitute.
2. Wear old boots so that you do not ruin your shoes.
3. Quietly observe the freshwater habitat. Observe the water's edge and peer through the water. Note sights and sounds.
4. Record and date your observations in your composition book.
5. Using the thermometer, determine the temperature of the water (Figure 1).

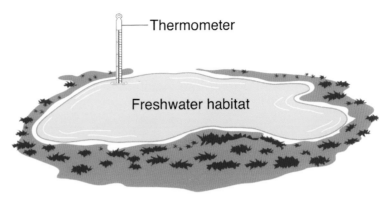

Figure 1

6. Record the temperature in your composition book.

7. Using the meterstick, determine the depth of the water (Figure 2). If it is deeper than 39 in. (1 m), you may need a tape measure.

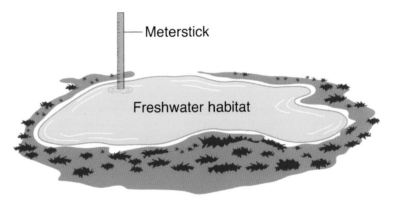

Figure 2

8. Record the depth in your composition book.

9. Place the float on top of the water near the water's edge. Mark the start location of the float.

10. Ten seconds later, mark the location of the float (Figure 3).

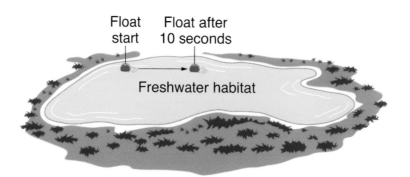

Figure 3

11. Measure the distance between locations.

12. Record the distance in your composition book. (Note: if the water is still, not moving, the float will not move much unless there is wind.)

13. Divide the distance by 10 seconds. This is the velocity of the moving water.

14. Test the water's pH by dipping a pH test strip into the water.

15. Record the results of the pH test in your composition book.

16. Fill the bucket with some water from the habitat.

17. Hold the larger net downstream, placing it against the bottom of the freshwater habitat, for a minute or two.

18. Bring up the net and gently deposit the contents into the bucket.

19. Observe the water and items in the bucket for life-forms.

20. Sketch in your composition book any living things you have found.

21. Refer to the pond field guide to attempt to identify as many of the organisms as possible. Also, count them, and record the number and the names of the organisms you have identified.

22. Return the organisms to the water in the habitat.

23. Using the large net again, disturb the bottom of the habitat.

24. Repeat steps 16 to 22.

25. Closer to the surface of the water or in still water, use the smaller nets and repeat steps 16 to 22 without touching the bottom of the habitat with your nets.

26. Clean up any trash you may have created.

 **Observations**

1. How many different types of organisms did you find?
2. Were you able to identify any of them?
3. Until performing this activity, were you aware of the biodiversity in that habitat?
4. What do you think would happen if the pH of the water changed or if contaminants were added to the water?
5. The following chart indicates what types of organisms are usually found depending on the water quality of a freshwater habitat. Based on the chart, how would you categorize the water quality of the habitat you just studied?

Good water quality	Fair water quality	Poor water quality
mayfly larvae	crayfish	aquatic worms
stonefly larvae	scud	leech
caddisfly larvae	dragonfly nymph	pouch snail
dobsonfly larvae	cranefly nymph	midge fly larvae
water penny	clam	blackfly larvae
riffle beetle	damselfly larvae	carp
trout	sow bug	
	catfish	

Note: Chart data are from http://school.discovery.com.

Our Findings

Please refer to the Our Findings appendix at the back of this volume.

Further Reading

"Gastropod." *The Columbia Encyclopedia*, 6th ed. 2008. Available online. URL: http://www.encyclopedia.com/doc/1E1-gastropo. html. Accessed October 18, 2010. Entry about a type of mollusk commonly found in fresh water.

Reid, G. *Pond Life: Revised and Updated*. New York: St. Martin's Press, 2001. Full-color guide to animals and plants that live in or near ponds.

Schultz, K. *Ken Schultz's Field Guide to Freshwater Fish*. Hoboken, NJ: Wiley, 2003. Field guide written by a renowned sportfisherman.

"Sculpin." *The Columbia Encyclopedia*, 6th ed. 2008. Available online. URL: http://www.encyclopedia.com/doc/1E1-sculpin.html. Accessed October 18, 2010. Entry about a type of fish commonly found in certain freshwater habitats.

Toupin, L. *Freshwater Habitat: Life in Freshwater*. Danbury, CT: Children's Press, 2005. Children's book about the organisms found in a freshwater habitat.

Weller, M. *Freshwater Marshes: Ecology and Wildlife Management*. Minneapolis: University of Minnesota Press, 1994. Advanced book that covers freshwater marshes from prairie potholes to wetlands.

20. STUDYING THE EFFECTS OF MOUNTAIN BARRIERS

Introduction

Mountains typically have vastly differing *climates* on their different sides. The rise of new mountains causes changes in climate. Those changes in turn directly impact both the *flora* and *fauna* of an area. For example, the rise of a mountain may cause desert conditions because rainstorms would now be blocked by the mountain range. The other side of the mountain, however, would receive all of the rainfall. The effects on the weather are so *profound* that there is a branch of *meteorology* devoted purely to mountains, known as mountain meteorology, which studies the effects of mountains on the *atmosphere*. The difference in climate can also lead to differences in *species* survival, which can lead directly to *speciation*. Humans living near mountains may have adopted specific *cultures* linked directly to the climate caused by the presence of mountain ranges.

In this experiment, you will create a model mountain range and observe the effects of barriers on climate.

Time Needed

45 minutes

What You Need

- Pyrex® baking dish
- rocks, several small and medium-sized
- paper cup

- food coloring
- measuring cup
- hot water, enough to fill the dish
- room temperature, water or cold enough to fill the dish
- pencil
- tape, a few pieces

Safety Precautions

Please review and follow the safety guidelines at the beginning of this volume. Exercise caution when handling hot water to avoid scalding.

What You Do

1. Using the pencil, poke and distribute 10 holes into the sides of the paper cup (Figure 1).

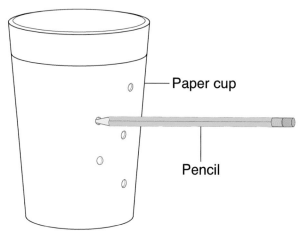

Paper cup

Pencil

Figure 1

2. Place the cup into one corner of the baking dish and tape it into place (Figure 2).

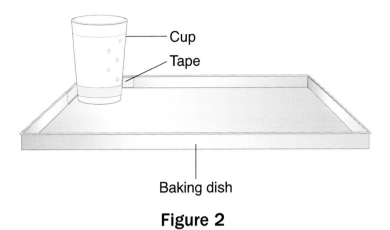

Figure 2

3. Line up and pile the rocks along the center of the dish, creating a "mountain range," but the pile should not be taller than the height of the dish (Figure 3).

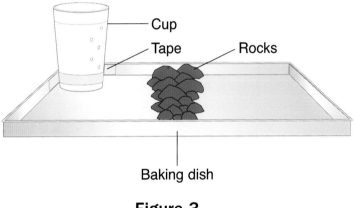

Figure 3

4. Add enough room temperature water to fill the dish and cover the rocks.

5. Add five drops of food coloring to 1 cup (240 ml) of hot water.

6. Pour the hot, colored water into the paper cup that is in the dish.

7. Observe what occurs.

8. Empty the water from the dish and cup.

9. Repeat steps 4 to 8, but add the hot, uncolored water to the dish, and add colored, cool water to the cup.

 **Observations**

1. Hot and cold air move similarly to hot and cold water. With that in mind, how do you think mountains might affect rainstorms and other types of weather?

2. How may the rise of a mountain range impact the land and wildlife around it?

3. There are several species of birds found only in Arabia. If the mountains of western Arabia were never formed, do you think these bird species would be living there? Without those mountains, how do you think the climate would have been affected and, in turn, the cultures of the people there?

Our Findings

Please refer to the Our Findings appendix at the back of this volume.

Further Reading

Alvarez, W. *The Mountains of Saint Francis: Discovering the Geologic Events That Shaped Our Earth*. New York: W. W. Norton, 2008. The man who discovered the great impact of an ancient asteroid discusses its effect on land, climate, and wildlife on Earth.

"Arabian Wildlife." Available online. *Arabianwildlife.com*. Accessed September 24, 2010. Provides photographs, information, and links about wildlife native to Arabian countries.

Gilligan, D. *In the Years of the Mountains: Exploring the World's High Ranges in Search of Their Culture, Geology, and Ecology*. Cambridge, MA: Da Capo Press, 2006. Told by a seasoned mountain climber, this book explores the world's highest mountains from a personal perspective.

Renner, J. *Mountain Weather: Backcountry Forecasting and Weather Safety for Hikers, Campers, Climbers, Skiers, and Snowboarders*. Seattle: Mountaineers Books, 2005. Information from a meteorologist on how to read weather patterns around mountains.

Scoggins, D. *Discovering Denali: A Complete Reference Guide to Denali National Park and Mount McKinley, Alaska*. Bloomington, IN: IUniverse, 2004. All-inclusive guide to Denali National Park, its landscape, and wildlife.

Uhler, J. "Denali National Park." 2007. Accessed September 24, 2010. Detailed information, including photographs and links about Alaska's Denali National Park, that describes Mt. Denali, the tallest mountain in North America.

Scope and Sequence Chart

This chart is aligned with the National Science Content Standards. Each state may have its own specific content standards, so please refer to your local and state content standards for additional information. As always, adult supervision is recommended (or required in some instances), and discretion should be used in selecting experiments appropriate for each age group or individual children.

Standard	Experiments
Unifying Concepts and Processes	all
Science as Inquiry	all
Physical Science	
Properties of objects and materials	1
Properties and changes of properties in matter	2
Position and motion of objects	
Motions and forces	
Light, heat, electricity, and magnetism	5
Transfer of energy	5
Life Science	
Structure and function in living systems	7, 9, 15, 18, 19
Life cycles of organisms	9, 18
Reproduction and heredity	
Regulation and behavior	7, 19

Organisms and environments	1, 6, 7, 9, 10, 15, 17, 19, 20
Populations and ecosystems	6, 7, 9, 10, 17, 18, 19, 20
Diversity and adaptations of organisms	6, 7, 9, 18, 19, 20
Earth Science	
Properties of Earth materials	1, 2, 3, 11, 13, 14
Structure of the Earth system	
Objects in the sky	
Changes in Earth and sky	3, 20
Earth's history	
Earth in the solar system	
Science and Technology	all
Science in Personal and Social Perspectives	
Personal health	8, 16
Characteristics and changes in populations	6, 7
Types of resources	1, 4, 13
Changes in environments	1, 2, 3, 9, 20
Science and technology in local challenges	1, 2, 12, 13, 16
Populations, resources, and environments	1, 20
Natural hazards	1, 2, 16
Risks and benefits	1, 2, 4, 12
Science and technology in society	1, 5, 8, 12, 13, 16
History and Nature of Science	all

Grade Level

Setting

The experiments are classified by materials and equipment use as follows:

- Those under SCHOOL LABORATORY involve materials and equipment found only in science laboratories. Those under SCHOOL LABORATORY must be carried out there under the supervision of the teacher or another adult.

- Those under HOME involve household or everyday materials. Some of these can be done at home, but call for supervision.

- The experiments classified under OUTDOORS may be done at the school or at the home, but require access to outdoor areas and call for supervision.

SCHOOL LABORATORY

8. Filtering Water to Prevent Pollution

16. Testing and Comparing Water Quality

HOME

1. Oils Spills and the Environment

2. Acid Rain

3. Slowing Down Erosion

6. Biodiversity Activity

7. Desert Adaptations and Water

9. Succession: Forest in a Jar

11. Soil Moisture and Permeability

13. Investigating Alternative Fuels (experiment is partially completed indoors)

15. Growing Plants Without Soil

17. Matching Animals to Their Biomes

OUTDOORS

Our Findings

1. OIL SPILLS AND THE ENVIRONMENT

1. Answers will vary but may include that the oil will stick to birds and plants, causing disease or death.

2. Answers will vary.

3. Answers will vary.

4. Answers will vary.

2. ACID RAIN

1. Since vinegar is an acid, the effects of vinegar will be similar to the effects of acid rain.

2. Answers will vary.

3. Answers will vary.

4. Answers will vary but may include that pollution not only affects air quality but also causes acid rain. Acid rain can fall anywhere on Earth and cause damage to buildings, rocks, plants, animals, and organisms in general.

3. SLOWING DOWN EROSION

1. The dish that contained only soil had more runoff.

2. The dish that contained soil and sod should have had more soil remaining.

3. The "men" were knocked down, modeling what could happen with large amounts of runoff causing flash flooding.

4. Grass and other plants keep the soil in place and prevent the soil particles form being carried off by the water.

5. Answers will vary.

4. WHAT NATURE RECYCLES

1. Answers will vary, but typically the paper bag will start to degrade.

2. Answers will vary.

3. When we use non-biodegradable products, we are harming the environment.

4. Answers will vary.

5. SOLAR STILL

1. The water was fresh water.

2. The buzzer did not sound, so there were no ions to conduct electricity; therefore, it was not salt water and had to be fresh water.

3. Answers will vary but may include tasting the water.

4. Solar stills are a natural, inexpensive method for distilling fresh water in areas where salt water may be plentiful but fresh water is not.

6. BIODIVERSITY ACTIVITY

1. The tropical rain forest had the greatest biodiversity.

2. The wheat field or lawn had the least biodiversity.

3. The items used to represent species show how many different species exist in a biome.

4. Not only are the trees of the rain forest important but also the rain forest is home to the greatest diversity of species. With the rain forests gone, all of those species will die.

5. We destroy habitats that can hold diversity and replace them with a low-diversity habitat. The species that lived in the natural habitat die out.

7. DESERT ADAPTATIONS AND WATER

1. The control sponge lost the most weight.

2. The sponges weighed less because the water evaporated.

3. Organisms in the desert must find ways to deal with the arid climate and prevent drying out.

4. Answers will vary.

8. FILTERING WATER TO PREVENT POLLUTION

1. Answers will vary.

2. If microorganisms were in the water, some sort of antibacterial additive or filtering would need to be added.

3. The polluted water will end up polluting the environment, killing other living organisms, and also potentially again ending up in our water sources.

9. SUCCESSION: FOREST IN A JAR

1. This is different from a terrarium because the purpose is to see how some plants will die out and be replaced by others.

2. Over time, plants that originally dominated the terrarium will die out as others take over, leading to a whole different set of organisms living there.

3. The excess water needed to disappear before they could grow.

4. A drier environment with some already sprouted bird seeds was necessary for the sunflower seed growth.

5. Answers will vary.

10. DANDELION'S HABITAT

1. Answers will vary.

2. Answers will vary.

3. Answers will vary.

4. Answers will vary.

11. SOIL MOISTURE AND PERMEABILITY

1. The sand sinks to the bottom because it is denser than the water.

2. The clay typically floats because of its lower density.

3. The potting soil typically remains suspended because of its lower density.

4. Potting soil is best for plant roots as the soil will allow water to remain below the surface but accessible to the roots.

5. Sand and clay would not hold the water the roots need to absorb.

12. CREATING A MODEL LANDFILL

1. Answers will vary.

2. Answers will vary.

3. Plants prevent water runoff and prevent the loss of soil that would uncover the garbage.

4. Answers will vary.

13. INVESTIGATING ALTERNATIVE FUELS

1. Answers will vary.

2. There were black particles on the filter paper.

3. We inhale them so they must affect our respiratory functions and cause diseases. Similarly, they can cause disease or death in other organisms. They can also destroy the habitats of organisms, also leading to their death.

4. Answers will vary.

14. DETERMINING SOIL QUALITY

1. Answers will vary.

2. Answers will vary.

3. Answers will vary.

4. The pots that held the plants that grew the tallest had the highest-quality soil.

5. Farmers can improve the quality and amount of their crops with higher-quality soil.

15. GROWING PLANTS WITHOUT SOIL

1. The sweet potato started growing a stem and roots. It was able to grow in the water because it had the nutrients it needed from the water and the potato itself.

2. The lima beans sprouted because they had water and used the stored nutrients in the beans.

3. They must be planted in soil because they have used up the stored nutrients in the potato/bean and now require nutrient rich soil to continue growing.

4. It would be useful to be able to grow plants without soil in areas where land is limited or the soil quality is poor.

16. TESTING AND COMPARING WATER QUALITY

1. Answers will vary.

2. Answers will vary.

3. Answers will vary.

4. The government must set limits to prevent harmful substances ending up in water in mass quantities.

17. MATCHING ANIMALS TO THEIR BIOMES

1. Answers will vary.

2. Answers will vary.

3. Answers will vary.

4. Answers will vary.

18. CREATING A LIVING BIOME

1. The plants can recycle the carbon dioxide and oxygen. The water evaporates and then condenses.

2. The plants provided a more natural habitat for the animal.

3. Answers will vary.

19. STUDYING A FRESHWATER HABITAT

1. Answers will vary.

2. Answers will vary.

3. Answers will vary.

4. There would be different organisms that would survive in that environment.

5. Answers will vary.

20. STUDYING THE EFFECTS OF MOUNTAIN BARRIERS

1. The weather systems will be affected the same way as when hot and cold air move.

2. The climate will change so the habitat will change, possibly causing the wildlife to die out; or the wildlife can no longer access the resources it needs and will die out.

3. Answers may vary but may include that the species would have been different if those mountains had never formed, since then the climate would be different.

Tips for Teachers

General

- Always review all safety guidelines before attempting any experiment.
- Enforce all safety guidelines
- Try the experiment on your own first to be better prepared for possible questions that may arise.
- You may try demonstrating each step of the experiment as you explain it to the students.
- Check for correlation to standards in order to best match the experiment to the curriculum.
- Provide adult assistance and supervision. Do not leave students unsupervised.
- Make sure students feel comfortable asking for help when needed.

Equipment and Supplies

- Most glassware can be purchased from scientific supply companies like Carolina Science Supply Company. Many companies have both print and online catalogs.
- Chemicals and special materials can also be purchased from these companies.
- Many of the supplies and substances used in the experiments are household items that can be found at home or purchased at a local market.
- For some of the hard-to-find items (e.g., extra-large jars), try asking local restaurants, or check warehouse-type stores that carry industrial-size items. For some substances (e.g., lamp oil), you should check with hardware or home-improvement stores.

Special-Needs Students

- Please make sure to follow the individualized education plans (IEPs) and 504 accommodation plans for any special-needs students.
- Provide a handout for students who require visual aids.
- Create a graphic representation of the experiment for students who use picture cards to communicate.
- For visually disabled students, provide copies with enlarged print.
- Involve students with dexterity issues by providing opportunities to participate in ways that match their abilities—e.g., be the timekeeper or the instruction reader.
- Read aloud directions for students who require verbal cues.

(continued)

- Record the instructions for playback.
- Repeat instructions more than once.
- Demonstrate the experiment so that students can see how it should be done correctly.
- Check frequently for comprehension.
- Ask students to repeat the information so that you can ensure accuracy.
- Break down directions into simple steps.
- Have students work with a lab partner or in a lab group.
- Provide adult assistance when necessary.
- Make sure that students with auditory disabilities know visual cues in case of danger or emergency.
- Simplify the experiment for students with developmental disabilities.
- Incorporate assistive technology for students who require it; e.g., use of Alphasmart® keyboards for recording observations and for dictation software.
- Provide preferred seating (e.g., front row) for students with disabilities to ensure they are able to see and hear demonstrations.
- Provide an interpreter if available for students with auditory disabilities who require American Sign Language.
- Consult with your school's inclusion specialist, resource teacher, or special education teacher for additional suggestions.
- Arrange furniture so that all students have clear access to information being presented and can move about the room (e.g., wheelchair-accessible aisles of about 48 inches).
- Offer students the option of recording their responses.
- Eliminate background noise when it is distracting.
- Face the class when speaking, and keep your face visible for students who lip-read.
- Repeat new words in various contexts to enhance vocabulary.
- Alter table heights for wheelchair access.
- Substitute equipment with larger sizes for easy gripping.
- Ask the student if he or she needs help before offering it.
- Place materials within easy reach of the students.
- Be aware of temperature. Some students may not be able to feel heat or cold and might injure themselves.
- Identify yourself to students with visual impairments. Also speak when you enter or leave the room.
- For visually impaired students, give directions in relation to the student's body. Do not use words like "over here." Also describe verbally what is happening in the experiment.

Glossary

A

accessible	easily obtained
acidic	containing acid-bearing pollutants
acid rain	precipitation that results from the combination of water and chemicals released into the atmosphere by the burning of fossil fuels
adapt	to adjust to different conditions
adaptations	alterations modified to fit a changed environment
adversely	opposing; confronting
alternative	other; as in a choice of two or more things
atmosphere	the air or climate of a specific place

B

bacteria	microorganisms made up of a single cell that has no distinct nucleus
biodegradable	capable of being decomposed by natural processes
biodiversity	the term that describes the number of different species that live within a particular ecosystem
biomes	a major regional or global community characterized chiefly by the dominant forms of plant life and the prevailing climate
brackish	having a somewhat salty taste; unpleasant
buoyancy	the power to float or rise in a fluid

C

carbon dioxide	a compound made up of molecules containing one carbon atom and two oxygen atoms, CO_2; normally found as a colorless, odorless gas that is exhaled by animals and absorbed by green plants
carbon monoxide	a compound made up of molecules containing one carbon atom and one oxygen atom, CO; usually formed when materials burn, such as in automobile exhaust
chloramine	any of a class of compounds obtained by replacing a hydrogen atom of an $-NH$ or $-NH_2$ group with chlorine; unstable, colorless, and derived from ammonia
chlorine	a chemical element, Cl, normally a corrosive gas, that is widely used for sterilization and cleaning

climate	a region's usual weather patterns
cognizant	fully informed; aware
communities	regions occupied by a group of interacting organisms
composition	makeup; structure
compounds	a substance containing two or more elements in definite proportions
condense	to make more dense or compact; to become liquid or solid
conserve	to keep constant
consumers	organisms, usually animals, that feed on plants or other animals
contaminants	impurities
contaminate	to make impure or unclean by contact or mixture
contamination	the act or making impure or unclean
crude oil	petroleum as it comes from the ground, before refining
cultures	the growing of microorganisms, tissue cells, or other living matter in a specially prepared manner

D

decay	decomposition; rot
deciduous forest	a type of forest characterized by trees that seasonally shed their leaves
desalination	the removal of salt from water, usually to make it drinkable
desert	a region of little rainfall that supports only sparse and widely spaced vegetation or no vegetation at all
deteriorates	disintegrates; wears away
devastating	destroying; overwhelming
devoid	completely lacking; empty
diesel	the type of gasoline designed to power a diesel engine
diligently	constant in effort to accomplish something
dispose	to get rid of
distilled	concentrated; purified
distinct	different in nature or quality; not identical
drought	a period of dry weather
dysentery	a painful disease of the intestines characterized by inflammation and diarrhea

E

ecological succession	the progressive replacement of one community by another

ecosystem	a collection of living things and the environment in which they live
elements	materials that cannot be broken down into simpler substances by normal chemical means
eliminated	removed; killed
endangered species	a species present in such small numbers that it is at risk of extinction
environment	the air, water, minerals, organisms, and all other external factors surrounding a given organism
environmental	relating to the environment
epiphytes	plants that grow on other plants, depending on them for structural support but not for nutrients
erosion	a type of weathering in which surface soil and rock are worn away through the action of glaciers, water, and wind
estuaries	a wide body of water formed where a large river meets the sea, containing both fresh and salt water
evaporate	to change from a liquid or solid state into vapor
evolved	changed by means of evolution

F

factors	elements contributing to a particular result
fauna	the animals of a given region or period, as a whole
flora	the plants of a particular region or period, as a whole
fossil fuels	coal, petroleum, and natural gas formed by the remains of plants and animals that lived millions of years ago
fragile	easily broken, damaged
fuels	substances consumed to produce energy

G

gas	a substance possessing the property of indefinite expansion; or a combustible fluid used as fuel, such as natural gas
genetic	affecting or determined by genes
geography	the study of the Earth and its physical characteristics, especially its surface features
global warming	the term attached to the notion that the Earth's temperature is increasing due to the greenhouse effect
gradually	changing evenly, or little by little
grasslands (savannah)	an area of grass or grasslike vegetation, characteristic of subhumid and semiarid climates
greenhouse effect	warming of the lower atmosphere caused by solar radiation being converted to heat due to the presence of certain gases in the atmosphere.

H

habitat   the natural environment of an organism

havoc   great destruction or devastation

hazardous   risky; dangerous

hydrogen ions   hydrogen of the form H^+, found in aqueous solutions of all acids

hydroponics   the cultivation of plants in an artificial environment in which the necessary nutrients are carried to the roots in a liquid mixture, rather than soil

hypothermia   abnormally low body temperature

hypothesize   to form a possible explanation for a natural phenomenon

I

impairing   growing or becoming worse; weakening

impede   to obstruct the progress of; hinder

insulate   to place in an isolated situation; segregate

L

landfill   a low area of land that is built up from deposits of solid waste in layers covered by soil

larvae   newly hatched, wingless, often wormlike forms of many insects before metamorphosis

lava flow   molten rock expelled by a volcano during eruption

leached   to dissolve out soluble components by percolation, or filtering

M

mammals   a class of vertebrates characterized by the production of milk by the females and, in most cases, by a hairy body covering; most newborn mammals emerge alive

marine   existing in or produced by the sea

meteorology   the study of weather and climate

microhabitats   a very small, specialized environment, such as a clump of grass or a space between rocks

N

nitrates   compounds containing the univalent group—ONO_2 or NO_3—as a salt or an ester of nitric acid

nitrites   compounds containing the univalent group NO_2, as a salt or an ester of nitrous acid

nitrogen   a chemical element, N, or more commonly found, N_2, that makes up about four-fifths of the atmosphere of the Earth, existing as a colorless, odorless gas

nitrogen oxide   any of several oxides of nitrogen formed by the action of nitric acid on oxidizable materials; present in car exhausts

non-renewable resource   resources—such as coal, oil, or natural gas—that take millions of years to form naturally and therefore cannot be replaced once they are consumed

nutrients   sources of nourishment

O

oil spill   an accidental release of oil into a body of water, as from a tanker, offshore drilling rig, or underwater pipeline, often presenting a hazard to marine life and the environment

opportunistic species   species that survive by the rapid colonization of a habitat; life is short, reproduction is high

orchids   any terrestrial or epiphytic plant of the family Orchidaceae, of temperate and tropical regions, having usually showy flowers, ranging from bluish to reddish purple

organism   a form of life composed of mutually interdependent parts that maintain various vital processes

overgrazing   feeding on growing grass in excess, to the detriment of the vegetation

ozone   a form of oxygen, O_3, produced when an electric spark or ultraviolet light is passed through air or oxygen

P

particulate   composed of distinct particles

permeability   the capability of a porous rock or sediment to permit the flow of fluids through its pore spaces

petroleum   a thick, flammable, yellow-to-black mixture of gaseous, liquid, and solid hydrocarbons that occurs naturally beneath the Earth's surface

pH   a measure of the strength of an acid or a base; neutral solutions have a pH of 7; acids, a pH between 0 and 7; bases, a pH from 7 to 14

phosphorus   a solid, nonmetallic element, P, that is used in forming smoke screens; its compounds are used in matches and phosphate fertilizers, and it is a necessary constituent of plant and animal life in bones, nerves, and embryos

photosynthesis   the use by green plants of the energy in sunlight to carry out chemical reactions, such as the conversion of carbon dioxide into oxygen; photosynthesis also produces sugars that feed the plant

physical environment	the way the world is and how it works
pollutants	things that contaminate air, soil, or water
polluted	contaminated
pollution	the introduction of harmful substances or products into the environment
population	all the individuals of one species in a given area
potassium	a silvery white metallic element, K, that oxidizes rapidly in the air and whose compounds are used as fertilizer and in very hard glasses
precipitation	falling products of condensation in the atmosphere, as rain, snow, hail, or a combination thereof
primary succession	the development of plant and animal life in an area without topsoil
profound	having deep insight or understanding, of deep meaning

R

rain forest	a tropical forest, usually of tall, densely growing, broad-leaved evergreen trees in an area of high annual rainfall
recycle	to use again, especially to reprocess
reefs	a strip or ridge of rocks, sand, or coral that rises to or near the surface of a body of water
reptiles	a class of scaly vertebrates that usually reproduce by laying eggs; lizards, snakes, turtles, and alligators are examples of reptiles
resources	sources of supply or support
roots	the usually underground portion of a plant that lacks buds, leaves, or nodes and serves as support, draws minerals and water from surrounding soil, and sometimes stores food
runoff	any precipitation that drains or flows off, like rainfall, not absorbed by soil, that flows off from the land in streams

S

salinity	the dissolved salt content of a body of water
scarce	absent or rare
secondary succession	the series of community changes that take place on a previously colonized but disturbed or damaged habitat, like a tree falling or a forest fire
sediment	mineral or organic matter deposited by water, air, or ice
silt	a sedimentary material consisting of very fine particles intermediate in size between sand and clay

solar still	an apparatus that uses solar radiation to distill salt or brackish water to produce drinkable water
solid	a substance having a definite shape and volume; one that is neither liquid nor gaseous
solution	a homogeneous mixture of two or more substances, which may be solids, liquids, gases, or a combination of these
speciation	the evolutionary formation of new biological species, usually by the division of a single species into two or more genetically distinct ones
species	a group of closely related and interbreeding living things; the smallest standard unit of biological classification
stomata	minute pores in the epidermis of a leaf or stem through which gases and water vapor pass
substances	physical matter or material
succession	the coming of one person or thing after another in order, sequence, or in the course of events
sulfur dioxide	a colorless, extremely irritating gas or liquid, SO_2, used in many industrial processes, especially the manufacture of sulfuric acid

T

taiga	vegetation composed primarily of cone-bearing, needle-leaved, or scale-leaved evergreen trees, found in regions that have long winters and moderate to high annual precipitation
tanker	a ship, airplane, or truck designed for bulk shipment of liquids or gases, usually a petroleum product
temperate (coniferous forest)	a forest in which there is enough rainfall to allow trees, shrubs, flowers, ferns, and mosses to flourish, while also following the rhythm of the seasons
terraces	a raised bank of earth having vertical or sloping sides and a flat top
terrestrial	living or growing on land; not aquatic
texture	the distinctive physical composition or structure of something, especially with respect to the size, shape, and arrangement of its parts
thrive	to prosper; flourish
topography	a graphic representation of the surface features of a place or region on a map, indicating their relative positions and elevations
toxins	poisonous substances, consisting mainly of protein, that are a by-product of metabolism in certain organisms
transported	taken or carried from one place to another
tsunami	an unusually large sea wave produced by a seaquake or an undersea volcanic eruption

tundra   a land area near the North Pole where the soil is permanently frozen a few feet underground

V

vegetation   the plants of an area or a region; plant life

vital   necessary to the continuation of life; life-sustaining

volcanic eruption the sudden occurrence of a violent discharge of steam and volcanic material

W

water vapor   water in a gaseous state, especially when diffused as a vapor in the atmosphere and at a temperature below boiling point

weathering   the process by which rocks are broken down into small grains and soil; it can happen through rainfall, ice formation, or the action of living things, such as algae and plant roots

wetlands   land that has a wet and spongy soil, as a marsh, swamp, or bog

wreak   to inflict or execute (punishment, vengeance, etc.)

Internet Resources

The Internet is a wealth of information and resources for students, parents, and teachers. However, all sources should be verified for fact, and it is recommended never to rely on any single source for in-depth research. The following list of resources is a sample of what the World Wide Web has to offer.

Access Excellence. "The National Health Museum." Available online. URL: http://www. accessexcellence.org. Accessed September 4, 2009. Resource for health teachers, including lessons and links.

American Rivers. "America's Most Endangered Rivers." 2010. Available online. URL: http://americanrivers.org/. Accessed July 14, 2010. Contains up-to-date news on rivers endangered by pollution as well as the efforts to preserve them.

BFI. "Sunshine Canyon Landfill." Available online. URL: http://www. sunshinecanyonlandfill.com/. Accessed September 8, 2009. Information provided by Browning-Ferris Industries regarding a landfill that they operate.

BP Global. "Gulf of Mexico Response." 2010. Available online. URL: http://www.bp.com. Accessed June 20, 2010. Information from the BP Web site about the world's largest ocean oil spill and the efforts to contain it.

Defenders of Wildlife. "Defenders of Wildlife." 2010. Available online. URL: http://www. defenders.org/. Accessed July 14, 2010. Web site of organization dedicated to preserving wildlife and providing information to the public about endangered animals.

Discovery Education. "Lesson Plans Library." Available online. URL: http://school. discoveryeducation.com/lessonplans. Accessed September 4, 2009. Lesson plans for teachers organized by grade level and content.

Duke University. "Forest Environment: Forest Succession." 2010. Available online. URL: http://www.dukeforest.duke.edu/forest/succession.htm. Accessed June 20, 2010. An article that explains how Duke Forest came into being through the process of succession.

Education.com. "The Parent's Guide to Middle School." Available online. URL: http:// www.education.com. Accessed September 6, 2009. Links for parents, teachers, and students on learning, self-esteem, subject areas, and a variety of topics.

The Educator's Reference Desk. "Lesson Plans." Available online. URL: http://www.eduref.org/Virtual/Lessons. Accessed September 5, 2009. Lesson plans for teachers arranged by content area.

Endangeredspecie.com "Endangered Species." 2002. Available online. URL: http://www.endangeredspecie.com/. Accessed July 14, 2010. List information about various currently endangered species as well as photographs of the animals.

Environmental Literacy Council. "Environment and Society." 2008. Available online. URL: http://www.enviroliteracy.org/category.php/5.html. Accessed July 14, 2010. Contains numerous links to articles explaining the link between society and the destruction of the environment.

Environmental Protection Agency. "Exploring Estuaries." 2009. Available online. URL: http://www.epa.gov/nep/kids/. Accessed July 14, 2010. Information geared toward children about estuaries, including interactive online games and activities.

Estuaries.gov. "Estuaries: Where Rivers Meet the Sea." 2010. Available online. URL: http://www.estuaries.gov/. Accessed July 14, 2010. Contains information, links, data, and interactive games about wildlife estuaries.

Genome.gov. "About Studying the Environmental Impact." 2010. Available online. URL: http://www.genome.gov/17516715. Accessed July 14, 2010. Discusses the impact of environmental factors on the human genome after exposure to various conditions.

Geography4kids.com. "Breaking it Down." Available online. URL: http://www.geography4kids.com/files/land_erosion.html. Accessed September 7, 2009. Explains erosion in simple terms for students.

Globio.info. "Globio." 2010. Available online. URL: http://www.globio.info/. Accessed July 14, 2010. Explains Globio, a framework used to model the impact of humans on the environment.

Grieve, M. "Dandelion." Botanical.com. Available online. URL: http://www.botanical.com/botanical/mgmh/d/dandel08.html. Accessed June 20, 2010. Detailed scientific information about the dandelion.

Groundwater Foundation. "Groundwater." 2010. Available online. URL: http://www.groundwater.org/?gclid=CKCY3ryY7KICFQdkgwodQGpIag. Accessed July 14, 2010. Official Web site of the Groundwater Foundation, dedicated to preserving the country's groundwater clean for future generations.

Hinrichsen, Don, and Bryant Robey. "Population and the Environment: The Global Challenge." 2002. Available online. URL: http://www.actionbioscience.org/environment/hinrichsen_robey.html. Accessed July 14, 2010. In excerpts from a Johns Hopkins University report, the authors explain evidence of how the environment is worsening.

Hotchalk. "Lesson Plans Page." Available online. URL: http://www.lessonplanspage. com. Accessed September 6, 2009. Lesson plans for teachers arranged by subject.

How Stuff Works. Available online. URL: http://home.howstuffworks.com. Accessed September 5, 2009. Explains in layman's terms how most machines and science-related concepts work.

Illinois Institute of Technology. "SMILE." Available online. URL: http://mypages.iit. edu/~smile/. Accessed September 5, 2009. Links to lessons for science and math teachers.

ITOPF. "Effects of Oil Spills." 2010. Available online. URL: http://www.itopf.com/marine-spills/effects/. Accessed June 20, 2010. Official Web site of the International Tanker Owners Pollution Federation Limited offers information on the environmental impact of oil spills.

McGinley, Mark. "Biome." *The Encyclopedia of Earth*. Available online. URL: http:// www.eoearth.org/article/biome. Accessed September 3, 2009. Provides information about the various types of biomes, their climates, and the organisms that live there.

National Geographic. "Acid Rain." 2010. Available online. URL: http://www. environment.nationalgeographic.com/global-warming/acid-rain-overview/. Accessed June 20, 2010. Contains color photographs and information about the environment impact of acid rain.

———. "Human Impact." 2009. Available online. URL: http://www.nationalgeographic. com/eye/impact.html. Accessed July 14, 2010. Includes links to information about how mankind has negatively impacted various habitats.

National Parks Conservation Association. "Wildlife Facts." 2010. Available online. URL: http://www.npca.org/wildlife_protection/wildlife_facts/. Accessed July 14, 2010. Explains how national parks contain some of the last habitats in existence for certain types of animals.

NOAA. "Office of Response and Restoration." 2010. Available online. URL: http:// www.response.restoration.noaa.gov.index.php. Accessed June 20, 2010. Up-to-date information from an official national agency tracking the response to the BP oil spill.

———. "Incident News." 2010. Available online. URL: http://www.incidentnews.gov. Accessed June 20, 2010. Contains links to daily updates to reports of oil spills off the coast of the United States, including the BP oil spill in the Gulf of Mexico.

North Valley Coalition. "Sunshine Canyon Landfill." Available online. URL: http://www. nodump.com/. Accessed September 8, 2009. A grassroots organization providing information to the public and documentation regarding the hazardous effects and alleged breaches of safety procedures at a dump in a residential neighborhood that was supposed to be shut down permanently.

"Puente Hills Landfill." Lacsd.org 2010. Available online. URL: http://www.lacsd.org/ about/solid_waste_facilities/puente_hills/default.asp. Accessed June 20, 2010. Official Los Angeles County Web site offering information about one of the county's landfills and its operations.

Science Daily. "Pollution News." 2010. Available online. URL: http://www.sciencedaily. com/news/earth_climate/pollution/. Accessed June 20, 2010. Includes news and links regarding pollution.

Shah, Anup. "Biodiversity." Global Issues. Available online. URL: http://www. globalissues.org/issue/169/biodiversity. Accessed September 7, 2009. Defines biodiversity and explains the impact we have on animal extinction.

United States Environmental Protection Agency. Available online. URL: http:// www.epa.gov/. Accessed September 7, 2009. Official government Web site with detailed information about the environment, policies and regulations related to the environment, and links to additional resources.

United States Geological Survey. Available online. URL: http://www.usgs.gov/. Accessed September 9, 2009. Official Web site for information pertaining to biology, geography, geology, geospatial information, and water of the Earth.

University of California Museum of Paleontology. "The World's Biomes." Available online. URL: http://www.ucmp.berkeley.edu/exhibits/biomes/index.php. Accessed September 3, 2009. Color photographs and details about the world's biomes.

U.S. Fish and Wildlife Service. "Endangered Species Program." 2010. Available online. URL: http://www.fws.gov/endangered/. Accessed July 14, 2010. Official government Web site with the capability to research different animals by state. Also explains what the federal government is doing to protect animals from extinction.

Wateruseitwisely.com. "Water Conservation Tips." 2009. Available online. URL: http:// www.wateruseitwisely.com/. Accessed July 14, 2010. Has information about how individuals can participate in conserving the world's water resources, starting in their own homes.

World Wildlife Federation. "Protecting the Future of Nature." 2010. Available online. URL: http://www.worldwildlife.org/species/. Accessed July 14, 2010. Web site of a foundation committed to the protection of wildlife species, containing information and photographs of different endangered species.

Index